EMBRACING THE GHOSTS

PTSD and the Vietnam Quagmire

J. Michael Orange

Foreword by
Cynthia L. Orange, award-winning author of "Shock Waves: A Practical Guide to Living With a Loved One's PTSD" and "Take Good Care: Finding Your Joy in Compassionate Caregiving"

All proceeds from the sale of this book will be donated to groups that help veterans and their families.

Cover photo by Michael Orange. The Minnesota Capitol Planning Board describes the "Monument to the Living" sculpture by Rodger M. Brodin, located on the Minnesota State Capitol grounds, as a "3.5 meter tall statue of hammered steel, portraying a nineteen-year-old soldier in full combat gear, asking a question that can be phrased a hundred different ways. For many of us it asks, 'Why do you forget us?'"

The statue was dedicated on May 22, 1982 during a time when society did not accord the respect to Vietnam veterans as has been the case since the 9/11/01 terrorist attacks.

We are what we think. All that we are arises with our thoughts. Speak or act with a pure mind and happiness will follow you as your shadow, unshakable. In this world, hate never dispelled hate. This is the law, ancient and inexhaustible.

THE BUDDHA

CONTENTS

For the members of my platoon in Vietnam whose names are on the Wall; and for Chris and Leo, whose names should be on the Wall. The war claimed their lives after they came home.

For the families, therapists, and healers who help us combat veterans reintegrate and mend, including Patrick Dougherty, Dianna Diers, Dr. Sean Hearn, Dr. Ken Druck, Claude AnShin Thomas, Rev. Rob Eller Issacs, and especially my therapist, Thomas.

To the Vietnamese people, including my friend, Mai Lee.

For my parents and my six brothers and sisters.

For Jessica and her family. The reciprocal love of our family enriches my life. Just the thought of all of you makes me smile.

For Cynthia. Since we married in 1973, I have become more we than me. It's a big improvement. You were my guiding light during my darkest days. My sanctuary. You saved my life, then reshaped it. I love you with my entire being.

AUTHOR'S NOTE

About the writing: With the exception of the names of my wife, Cynthia, and our daughter, Jessica, and people who preferred to be named, I have changed all of the names of non-public individuals to respect their privacy. I have reconstructed and reimagined conversations based on the voluminous notes I took throughout my therapy for post-traumatic stress disorder (PTSD) and my memory. Each of us are authors of our memories.

About the readers: I hope this book will be useful for anyone who has lived with their own or a loved one's trauma as well as for those healers who guide trauma survivors out of the darkness. For those who live with someone with PTSD, my wife's book can serve as an extremely helpful companion: *Shock Waves: A Practical Guide to Living with a Loved One's PTSD*, by Cynthia Orange.

About military service: I have great respect for our military and for those who have served. I have spoken countless times to students about my military experiences. I usually say that if I could guarantee that service in our armed forces would only involve the actual defense of this country or joint peace-keeping missions as part of the United Nations, I would urge every able-bodied student to serve. I also tell them that, unfortunately, there can be no such guarantee. Since World War Two and Korea, our leaders have used our military might primarily for the same reasons powerful countries have done throughout history—in pursuit of power, ego, and resources.

This book is about the moral injury that results from moral service in an immoral war.

In *Embracing the Ghosts*, Michael Orange presents a deeply-toned mosaic, a "re-membering," of exiled parts of the life and memory that brought him to psychotherapy, meditation, political activism, and elderhood.

Met with much honesty, humility, courage, and compassion, the ghosts reveal their lessons to Michael and to us. It is not what or even who we are, but how we are with all of ourselves and one another that heals.

—Dianna Diers, MA, LMFT, psychotherapist and
grief counselor

Michael's openness and honesty about his life experiences make a compelling story of what it means to carry war within one's self. Like so many other combat veterans, he tried to minimize the effects that war and its atrocities had on him. However, through therapy, he learned that trauma can't be "wished away" or ignored. He also discovered that trauma is cumulative—how growing up in a dysfunctional family plagued by alcohol exacerbated his combat PTSD.

Fortunately, Michael also found that trauma is a burden that needn't be carried alone if you have the courage to ask for help. He was fortunate to have his compassionate wife, Cynthia, and a supportive family and community that listened without judgment and held him along his path of introspection and healing.

—Michael P. McDonald, teacher, community leader,
and President of Chapter 27, Veterans For Peace

War is a virus—a shadow that lingers like singed smoke that seeps into our darkest dream world. Many of us have been touched by its malevolence. Those of us who don't kill ourselves, struggle to build steps out of our basement of feelings and memories, but usually don't have a plan to guide us.

Michael Orange's book offers the steps he used to find his way out. He shares his stories, his path, and his building materials within its pages. Michael is a survivor who now stands on the shore of darkness, holding high his light to help us so we can find our own way home. Thank you, for your courageous book. It is written with love and is a true guide towards healing.

—Chante Wolf served 12 years in the U.S. Air Force including deployment to Saudi Arabia in support of Desert Shield/Storm in 1991. Her war journal was published in *The Veterans Book Project: Objects for Deployment*. Other writings, photography and her military story have been published in: *Costs of Freedom: An American Anthology of Activism; the Compassionate Rebel Revolution; War Fever Syndrome; The Pulse; Southside Press; Veterans Today Journal; Veterans For Peace; Meat for Tea; Main Street Rag* and *MN Women's Press*.

It's not by accident that this is not Michael's first book about Vietnam. His first captures the horrors and wounds of war; *Embracing the Ghosts* describes his path to healing. As he so poignantly shows us, trauma is an ongoing journey. But, with the appropriate tools and support, it is a journey that can lead to self-awareness, inner strength, and joy. All of us—especially those affected by PTSD—can take great hope in that.

—Sean T. Hearn, M.D.

REVIEWS

In *Embracing the Ghosts*, Michael Orange brings to light the reality that within each of us exists all past generations. He skillfully demonstrates the necessity of waking up not only to this truth but to the truth of cause and effect—that no action, no experience, exists without consequences. Orange shows us that healing is possible, but that healing is not the absence of suffering. Healing means developing the ability to live at peace with our un-peacefulness. As we heal, we not only heal for all past generations but for the whole, interconnected world of which we are a part.

—Claude AnShin Thomas, Vietnam combat veteran,
Zen monk, and author of *At Hell's Gate:
A Soldier's Journey from War to Peace*

When Michael Orange reentered the world after serving in Vietnam, he struggled for decades to suppress the horror and memories of what he had experienced. But trauma was always present, tugging on his sleeve like an insistent child that demands attention. When he could no longer outrun or hide from the reality of PTSD, he finally got the professional help he so desperately needed. *Embracing the Ghosts* is his journey of healing.

But it is much more. With vulnerable honesty, Orange describes how, with a wise therapist as his guide, he was able to plumb the depths of personal history to understand how painful childhood experiences and the unmet need for parental approval shaped and directed his life choices. He was only 13 when he left home for seminary boarding school. At 19, he followed in his father's footsteps and joined the Marines. With intense therapy, the research of experts, and genuine support, Orange found permission and encouragement to heal the wounded child within so he could then heal the wounds of war and trauma.

By so generously sharing his own story, Orange, in turn, offers others who struggle with PTSD, grief, and the confusion that comes with childhood neglect, that same permission to courageously face—and ultimately embrace—their own ghosts. *Embracing the Ghosts* is a remarkable book of hope and a reliable roadmap for healing.

—Ken Druck, Ph.D., executive coaching/consulting, and author of several books including, *Raising an Aging Parent, Courageous Aging, The Real Rules of Life*, and co-author of *The Secrets Men Keep: Breaking the Silence Barrier*

As Michael Orange so adeptly demonstrates in his book *Embracing the Ghosts*, a principal goal of trauma therapy for veterans is to help them accept how their military experiences affected them and to have compassion for themselves as they do the hard work of healing. With courage and honesty, Orange has created a "How To" manual of how he achieved that goal.

But *Embracing the Ghosts* is not just for combat veterans. This is a book for *anyone* with a history of trauma, as well as for their loved ones who too often suffer in silent helplessness as their partner or parent or child or dear friend struggle with PTSD. Through engaging stories and helpful advice of experts, Orange unflinchingly describes how he traveled from suppression to understanding, and finally being able to embrace his trauma *ghosts* as valuable teachers.

—Patrick Dougherty, M.A., L.P., clinical psychologist, Qigong teacher, a former Marine and combat veteran of the Vietnam war whose work is now focused healing the collective trauma of war. He is the author of *A Whole-Hearted Embrace, Finding Love at the Center of It All* and *Qigong in Psychotherapy: You can do so much by doing so little.*

ACKNOWLEDGMENTS

It is well said regarding accomplishments that we stand on the shoulders of those who came before us. It's also true for writing a book. I stand on the shoulders of so many people; all of them long-time friends with whom I would feel privileged to share and defend a foxhole.

My dear friend since 1977, Rick Slettehaugh, guided me on the early drafts of this book as he did so expertly and patiently with my prior book, *Fire in the Hole*. Another dear friend, Vince Hyman, a man with a professional command of the English language, prodded me, page by page, to write a better book, to go deeper. And David Morris, a man whom the late U.S. Senator Paul Wellstone told me was, "The smartest person he ever met," a man whom I've admired since I met him in 1984, dug into a later draft and helped me pull out this more evolved result.

My siblings helped me be fully honest about our shared upbringing. Their memories complemented mine, and a fuller depiction of our family dynamics emerged. I hope this will help the reader appreciate the important role that childhood issues can play during therapy for PTSD.

I get compliments on my prior book, *Fire in the Hole,* and my stock answer is that I have a terrific editor—the incredible woman I married in 1973—whose fingerprints are on every page. My stock answer holds true for this book too. It's not an easy author-editor relationship. Entire stories die with the push of her delete key and whole pages rearrange. But since she has published five books, two of them national award winners, and edited many more, I have learned to welcome her wise transformations. My drafts needed her word alchemy like a raw clay vase needs the kiln to become watertight.

FOREWORD

Remembering All Those Scarred by War
by Cynthia Orange

Years ago, my husband, daughter, and I visited the Vietnam Memorial in Washington D.C. It struck me as a large, dark, wing of death carved into the earth with names of fallen soldiers etched into the smooth granite in the order in which they died. Jessica and I stood at each end of 1969-1970, Michael's tour of duty, and I was taken aback by the enormity of loss.

These losses are tragic, but they are tangible, even touchable when you have a memorial. But what about the other casualties of war whose names will never be carved on the memorials we visit—those scarred by war who far outnumber the war dead? What about my husband and the multitude of wounded warriors who didn't die but who carry their trauma and emotional scars deep within?

Or what about Kevin and Joyce Lucey, who sign their emails, "The proud parents of Cpl. Jeffrey Michael Lucey, a 23-year-old USMC reservist forever. Succumbed to the hidden wounds of PTSD on 06/22/04." When Jeff came back from Iraq, he often got drunk in an attempt to numb the pain, and VA said they couldn't help him until he was alcohol-free.

Feeling helpless, Kevin and Joyce watched their son fall apart, becoming as hyper-vigilant as trauma survivors. They hid knives and took away anything they thought Jeff might use to harm himself. One night, just before midnight, Kevin said Jeff asked him for the second time in ten days if he could sit on his dad's lap and rock him like he used to when Jeff was little. The next day Kevin came home to discover that even their fierce love could not quell the horrors of war. His son had hung himself. "I held Jeff one last time as I lowered his body from the rafters," he said through his tears.

I remember telling a friend that I felt lost in the "bewilderness" when Michael was finally diagnosed with post traumatic stress disorder (PTSD). It took many years (and many therapy sessions) to understand that I, as the caring spouse of a Vietnam veteran with PTSD, had a need—and a right—to also grieve what we have lost, individually and as partners. Grief is a messy process, and despite all the books and discussions about "stages," it is usually non-linear, and feelings can wash over me at unexpected times. Like when I visit a memorial, or try to comfort my husband when he wakes shaking from a nightmare.

War changes us forever—all of us: veterans, spouses, children, healers, and citizens. I know the trauma and ghosts of war will always be with Michael—which means they will be with me too. Ernest Hemingway wrote, "The world breaks everyone and afterward, many are strong at the broken places." I give thanks that we grew stronger. We will soon celebrate our 47th anniversary, and each year our marriage continues to grow sweeter, more solid, and more realistic because we know what we almost lost.

Embracing the Ghosts is a poignant reminder that we must never forget all the victims of war—those for whom the only escape was suicide, the loved ones like the Luceys who grieve in suicide's wake; those with PTSD like Michael, who forever carry the weight of war; and those loved ones who struggle to help lift that heavy burden. It is our sacred duty to give all these lives and stories meaning.

Michael honors that duty each and every day in his work in the world, his veterans' service work, his commitment to peace, to social, economic, and environmental justice. He is a dedicated and amazing partner, father, father-in-law, and the most joy-filled grandfather I have ever seen. With this book, he has given a great gift to all who seek to understand the complexities of trauma and the importance of therapy. It is testament to resilience, a beacon of hope, and pathway to healing. I love this man beyond measure, and it is a privilege to share this life with him.

Cynthia Orange (www.cynthiaorange.net) is a writer, editor, and writing consultant. Her most recent award-winning books include *Take Good Care: Finding Your Joy in Compassionate Caregiving* and *Shock Waves: A Practical Guide to Living With a Loved One's PTSD.*

Cynthia Orange co-facilitates a group for caregivers of a variety of ages and circumstances that was founded in 2010, and she and her husband often speak to audiences about the effects of trauma and war in their continuing involvement with veterans and veterans' issues.

PREFACE

I cannot unlive my life. I was a soldier. I came home. I learned more than I wanted to about the boil of silence.
— Tim O'Brien, *Dad's Maybe Book*

I have used this writing process to follow Socrates' ancient aphorism to "know thyself," to reflect on my life, affirm what others mean to me, articulate what I stand for, and tell stories that illustrate the evolution of my core beliefs. There have been four critical influences in my life: childhood, my four years in a Catholic seminary during high school, Vietnam, and my adult life with my wife, Cynthia and daughter, Jessica, and now with our son-in-law and two adorable grandchildren.

Two years after leaving the relative sanctuary of a Catholic seminary high school, I joined the Marines fully aware in 1968 that the decision would likely send me to Vietnam. Little did I know that the weight of that decision would last a lifetime. For thirty-three years, I attempted to stuff the images, memories, and effects of combat, but America's War on Terror reenergized the ghosts I constantly tried to outrun. When my psychic crashes became intolerable, I began therapy in 2003 and was diagnosed with post-traumatic stress disorder (PTSD). My long overdue journey of healing began.

Since I have already written about my experiences during the war in my book, *Fire in the Hole: A Mortarman in Vietnam*, this writing can serve as a bookend to those stories.

Embracing the Ghosts describes the circumstances that led to my decision to enlist and the therapy I completed so many years later. While my story has elements common to many who join the military to serve their country and then suffer the scars from that decision, it will resonate with anyone who has lived with their own or a loved one's trauma as well as with those healers who guide trauma survivors out of the darkness.

Memories. Sometimes it seems fifty years ago; sometimes just yesterday. They have mass like heavy stones in a backpack. Writing them down lightened my load. How I live the present defines my future. Combat is not a normal part of the human experience. The disorder part of the PTSD diagnosis is a reasonably sane response to the insanity of war.

It was through my therapy that I learned how to deal methodically and compassionately with the trauma of my wartime experiences. Therapy also gave me permission to acknowledge that while combat resulted in my PTSD, unresolved childhood issues exacerbated matters. The therapy process enabled me to see the spins I put on it over the years, the delusions, and to embrace and learn from all of my life lessons.

Writing it down is a freeing experience. It helps me be informed by my past, not imprisoned by it. My present life is richer and more authentic when I embrace my past and all of the people involved (including myself) with compassion. I hope you, my reader, can draw your own useful lessons from it.

INTRODUCTION

My tour of duty in Vietnam (1969-1970) produced a case of post-traumatic stress disorder (PTSD) that I now know is very typical for Vietnam combat vets. The effort necessary to realize this took half a lifetime and excessively taxed the patience and compassion of the people closest to me, especially my wife, Cynthia, and daughter, Jessica. Since I had health care from my employer, I sought out a private psychotherapist (I call him Thomas) instead of using the VA's group therapy services. My course of talk therapy (which didn't include the use of drugs) ran forty-four sessions over a nine-month period that started in April of 2003. With a meticulousness birthed in the excellent education my parents and the Catholic Church provided me as a youth, I faithfully made typewritten notes after each session, over one hundred pages that covered each of the fifty-minute sessions as well as what I was thinking, reading, and feeling during that intense time.

By our third session, Thomas reached his diagnosis, and the VA agreed six months later that I was partially disabled due to combat-induced PTSD. "PTSD expressed by agitated depression, emotional flooding, intensive traumatic recollections, feelings of detachment and estrangement from others, sense of foreshortened future, difficulty concentrating, chronic stress and fear of physical and emotional breakdown." This was Thomas's diagnosis. I didn't realize how screwed up I was and wondered if there was a 32-word cure for this 32-word conclusion.

Parts I-IV focus on the trials and lessons learned from my PTSD therapy, including the prior conditions and trauma that greatly influenced my combat experiences. Part V includes a selection of essays that describe meeting my Cynthia in 1968, finding a spiritual home in humanism, five lighthearted stories that involve my father, and a final story about paying-it-forward by performing at the Minnesota Veterans Home.

My well-aged brain provides an analogy that describes the value of all of this writing: Troubling aspects of my past are like the things I need to do before some big event. Items on the list will bounce around in my head and distract me like an irritating husk of popcorn stuck in a tooth while I repeatedly struggle to recall the entire list. The resulting anxiety spoils the present and taints the future event. Writing things down stores them to an external hard drive that frees up room on my brain's very limited hard drive so I can be more present.

As part of my therapy, I did a lot of research into the effects of growing up in a dysfunctional family and combat-induced PTSD. I summarize this information in Parts I-IV and also included longer citations from the most important books in the Appendix at the back of the book. In the Resources section, also at the end of the book, I include the symptoms of PTSD and a list of helpful resources.

PART I

Into the Quagmire

Prelude 1: "I Married the War"
(from an essay Cynthia Orange wrote in 2000)

When I married Michael, I soon discovered I had also married Vietnam. In the early days and long nights of our marriage, the ghosts of Vietnam often slept between us, preventing caresses. Even then, before all the knowledge of post traumatic stress was common, I intuitively knew it was important for him to talk about Vietnam. I was safe and love him unconditionally, fiercely, protectively. Back then, he would talk to no one else, and didn't even want new acquaintances to know he was a Vietnam vet.

I tried to ease his burden by sharing it, by listening to his stories. As I listened, I ached from the weight of that terrible war. My eyes stung from the smoke of burning villages, my body rocked back and forth with the peasants as they hugged themselves tight in their grief. I still remember the name of the little cat -- *Titi Lau*, that got eaten by the rats. I walked in jungle heat in dreams, saw little boys get cut to pieces after they planted a homemade bomb, smelled the pieces of their flesh as it floated down around me.

Even as a little girl, our daughter knew to be careful not to startle her dad, not to wake him suddenly. As an adult, she has written poignant poems about this, about how they protected each other from his dark dreams and memories. He used to dream about Vietnam a lot, almost every night when we were first married. I'd lay close, matching my breathing to his own, waiting until his breaths seemed smooth, his sleep restful.

We have a good life and a great partnership. Michael's "it's a good day; no one's shooting at me. . ." attitude has rubbed off, and I am blessed to be sharing my life with him. He no longer dives for cover when he hears a car backfire, and he has learned about the danger of silences. Two of our dear friends have been diagnosed with post-traumatic stress disorder, and we live in fear that the war might kill them yet.

Some years ago, Michael worked up the courage to begin speaking to elementary, junior high, and high-school students about his experiences. Each time I hear him do this, my heart cracks a little more, but his is healing. At times like this I understand my mother a little better when she hushed my father after he started telling one of his World War Two stories.

Michael began writing about Vietnam several years ago. As his stories move from catharsis to craft, he says he moves further from the raw emotion. He shows me the stories and asks me to edit them, "to make them better." I respond as a teacher and offer concrete advice. But as a wife, a lover, a best friend, my insides churn as I am again taken to the sights, smells, tastes, sounds and feelings of Vietnam. I want so desperately to "make it better," to kiss the wounds, erase the pain.

For those of us—and I suspect there are millions—who have connected so intimately with our veterans that we begin to feel the phantom pain of their severed limbs, there is little chance of forgetting. We have learned to love the warrior and not the war, but the war still haunts us every day.

Prelude 2: Dream Workshop

Like every combat vet I ever met, I've been plagued by nightmares. At the recommendation of a friend, I read Dr. Jeremy Taylor's book, *Where People Fly and Water Runs Uphill*. Taylor was a dream therapist who, for nearly forty years before his death in 2018, helped countless people learn from their dreams. I now see my dreams as plays my subconscious stages for my benefit. Like any faithful lover of the theater, I have to work to understand what my personal playwright is trying to convey. I have dreamed all of the classics that are as old as our species, but always fresh with each revival: "I'm Naked but Nobody Notices," or "I'm Flying in the Air or Under Water," or "I Have to Pee but Can't Find a Toilet."

For nearly three decades, the theater of my dreams was haunted by my experiences in the theater of war in Vietnam. I staged repeat performances of classics like "Someone's Trying to Kill Me," and its chilling sequel, "I'm Killing Someone."

Taylor's book helped me accept the truth of his assertion that "there is no such thing as a bad dream," and that "all dreams come in the service of health and wholeness, and speak a universal language of metaphor and symbol."[1]

Just before I began my PTSD therapy, a fellow Vietnam vet and I organized a special workshop for veterans with Dr. Taylor. The night before the workshop, I followed the advice in his book and set my mind to remember my dream in the morning. And then I wrote it down.

It was a new staging of an old and very familiar theme: My special place of sadness. My starring role was as the antihero. My subconscious director only let me remember the last act. It opened at one end of an earthen amphitheater. I was at the lowest part and to my right and left, military troops closely packed both of the up-sloping sides. Dressed totally in black like a SWAT team, they trained their rifles on a huge dark opening in the amphitheater's banks that loomed in front of me. I thought of the overwhelming strategic advantage of their fields of fire over any adversary that came from the dark opening. Their elevation above the target zone would allow crossfire without risk of friendly fire. I was in a tight-fitting military uniform too but it was all blue, not black, and I was unarmed. Others, also dressed in the blue uniform, packed in around me.

I turned towards the dark maw, and a phalanx of black-uniformed troops close-marched out—six abreast and about twenty deep—with their rifles slung over their shoulders. Behind them came a motley group of civilians, male and female of all ages, shapes, and multi-colored attire. Like the troops, they were close-packed, but walked as individuals with hurried starts and stops. Many carried peace and antiwar protest signs. I remembered thinking how they lacked the disciplined appearance and strength, and the coordinated action of the troops that filled the amphitheater. The dream played on to the next scene as if I knew what was going to happen but could spare no emotional response to it. The air exploded with the sharp reports from hundreds of high-powered rifles. Bullets from both sides ripped through bodies tall and short. Like a rain-pelted lake, blood spattered up from the small crowd of demonstrators.

The protestors in front of me absorbed round after round, I instinctively knew my role this time. A tall protestor close to me threw his head up and to the left towards me as his chest exploded. Even with a grimace, I recognized him as John, a friend from boot camp. His sign arched into the air above his head and he twisted to his left and began to double over. I quickly moved in and he slowly draped himself over my right shoulder as his blood and life oozed out of him. With a smooth fluidity of motion, I carried his body fireman style down a long dark hallway underground. When I came to some stairs, an obese woman ahead of me slowed my progress to a crawl as she labored her way up the stairs. I thought of asking to go around her, aware of the blue-collar rule that the person with a load has the right-of-way, but realized there was not room to do so. John's body was very light, so patience was an easy choice. At the top of the stairs was an airport-style moving walkway that carried me into a massive airplane hangar.

The hanger had no planes. Instead, two men dressed in white lab coats stood astride a large enameled-metal table. As I approached, I overheard them chuckling over something. When they turned to beckon me, I saw the blood splatters that caked the fronts of their lab coats.

"The last plane left," one of the men explained. "There'll be another one soon. Put him face-down there on the table." As I dutifully laid John's body where he had pointed, I noticed that the other man was flipping through what appeared to be medical charts. He seemed disconnected, not disrespectful, just aloof.

I turned to the first man and said, "I want to see his face," then burst into tears as the first very familiar wave of emotional sadness rolled over me.

"You can't." The answer was flat and unmovable.

I repeated my request as I knelt down in front of the table. I clasped my hands on top of the table as if in prayer, and convulsed with sobs. Both men leaped to my sides and, with hands protected in latex gloves, wrenched my hands from the bloodied tabletop. The last emotion I felt before the curtain dropped on my dream play was anger at these two men. I wanted that blood on my hands. I carried into my awake life that very familiar feeling; that here-we-go-again feeling of overwhelming sadness.

I told this dream that evening to Dr. Taylor and the sixteen veterans who attended the dream workshop. Mine was the last one we discussed and it sparked quite the discussion. Many of the vets made comments on the military aspects of the dream and death of the peace protestors.

The real knock-me-over comment came from a fellow Marine and Vietnam combat vet around my age, a psychologist and therapist named Thomas. "The large woman is of interest to me," he began. "If it was my dream, I think she's saying to me, 'You're not getting past me with that burden. You have to deal with me first.'"

It rang true, and the "aha" sensation really gave me the tingle of truth.

Thomas asked about the friend I mentioned, John. "A few years ago, I traced his name on a black granite wall in D.C." I replied. "A bouncing betty took him out a few months into his tour of duty." Thomas gave me a look filled with warmth and compassion; a look that communicated, "I know. I understand, because I've lived this." And I knew then and there I wanted him to be my therapist.

1. MY PTSD STORY: A STORY OF TRAUMA AND RECOVERING

(Excerpts from this story were published in *The Veteran*, Vietnam Veterans Against the War: "My Personal Journey with PTSD," Fall 2008 and "Walkin' the Talk (Therapy)," Fall 2017. The Appendix includes the symptoms of PTSD.)

War is so unjust and ugly that all who wage it must try to stifle the voice of conscience within themselves.
> — Leo Tolstoy, *War and Peace*,

War is necrophilia
> —Chris Hedges, *War is a Force that Gives Us Meaning*,

Military power is just as corrupting to the man who possesses it as it is pitiless to its victims. Violence is just as devastating to the soul of the perpetrator as it is to the body and souls of those who are victims of it.
> —American Friends Service Committee

Dammit! It's into the pit again. I feel it like a ground fog with claws. If the feeling could have substance and mass, it would be a dark, lifeless mud that sucks you down. The descent triggers a flashback to endless nights in a foxhole while the roaring waterfall of monsoon rains isolates all contact with my fellow Marines and drowns all hope of relief in an eroding water torture. Frozen by emotional quicksand, I shiver uncontrollably in the bone-chilling cold—or is it the sobbing? The mud here drains the body's warmth and energy.

How can I be so snivelingly weak? How could I have been such a spineless coward? What is this place? Why am I here? Why am I so tired? Why are the shattered bodies here with me? When will it end? Why can't I stop crying? Cold.

My left foot pulsated with a piston-like throb that matched the beat of the heart that powered it. Fight or flight? Calming breaths from decades of yoga and meditation practice proved only marginally effective. The second-floor waiting room served several offices tucked into a century-old, brick office building that fronted on a quiet street in a not-yet-gentrified neighborhood in St. Paul. It was 8:50 on a Tuesday morning. A drink from the water cooler for my parched mouth was a helpful distraction. I thought back on how the decision two weeks earlier to go to the Minneapolis Veterans Affairs Medical Center had led to this moment. I sensed that stepping through the door opposite me into the therapist's office would start a journey back into the memory abyss of Vietnam and its tangles of suffocating jungles and confounding emotions. I didn't know it would be that and so much more.

"Please, come in and sit down," Thomas said as he motioned toward a simple cushioned chair just beyond the swing of the door. He looked taller than I first thought when I met him two weeks ago at the dream workshop. He was my average height but so thin, especially in the face, and his receding hairline was winning the race to capture his balding head. The office was small; intimate, but not claustrophobic. Early morning sunlight streaming in the sole, double-sash window, filtered through plants of all sizes and shapes, and cast a warm glow on photos of his wife and two sons. A statue of the Buddha partially hid his psychology degree and psychologist's license propped up unobtrusively on a shelf. Books filled every remaining available space. It was a comfortable space, a secure place from which to burrow back into the dark and dangerous past and grapple with questions I didn't want asked.

Thomas sat in a simple armless office chair opposite me at a distance that I knew from my architecture training to be balanced; not so far as to seem remote and not too close as to feel intrusive. He slipped off his shoes and effortlessly gathered his willowy legs into a full lotus position. Looking up and directly at me, a slight smile revealed a mouth full of perfect teeth that overwhelmed his attentive face. An inscrutable Buddha himself. I came to know him as a man of few words who rarely showed surprise. A focused deliberateness about his every move and word fit more his moonlighting job. He also teaches qigong, an ancient Chinese meditative art. Later he told me that he was raised Catholic and considers himself a "Taoist with Catholic leanings." His forte, I soon learned, is the ability to combine Western psychotherapy with Eastern philosophy and meditative practice. I immediately noticed an intensity in his eyes that his wire-rimmed glasses softened only a little; perhaps a vestige of the thousand-yard stare he developed as a Marine grunt walking the point in Vietnam. We had walked the same walks and could talk the same talk. The journey back began.

Before The Crash

"Let's start with the things that brought you into this office," Thomas began after we had taken care of the formalities and paperwork. "Have you sought treatment at the VA?" I told him that three and a half years after coming home, I was really struggling with nightmares, startle response, and bouts of sadness. At Cynthia's urging (we had recently married), I checked in at the Minneapolis VA Medical Facility. While I sat waiting in a hallway, I noticed vet after vet passing by limping or missing limbs, or sitting nearby with feet drumming on the floor and heads slumped over. I didn't feel worthy of help. I fled, embarrassed to seek help for my invisible injuries.

"What happened recently that led to your being here this morning?" I was not sure how far back to go. "Pick any point in time," Thomas softly assured me. "A correct chronology is not too important at this stage." He shifted his pose slightly as if settling in for a retreat-level meditation.

"Well … things … things just sorta' piled up on me," I stammered.

"Just pick one to start with," Thomas said encouragingly.

I started to tell him the story about Chris, my best friend in Vietnam, but it quickly became convoluted, as is the nature of my life and memories. At this stage in our therapy journey, Thomas rarely steered me back on a course he thought more appropriate but rather let me muddle my way through the telling. He was actively finding the connective themes for my many waypoints.

"Chris was a very good man," I began. "I learned from his family that he died about ten years ago in a car accident." I explained that I had published a book about my Vietnam experiences two years earlier (*Fire in the Hole: A Mortarman in Vietnam*) and it included the story of Chris's key role in a friendly fire incident. Thomas said that rather than read about this story in my book, he'd rather I tell it to him. I gave him the Reader's Digest version of the confluence of three mistakes, one of which was mine, that resulted in the critical wounding of three Marines, one of whom later died.

"Chris saved my ass that night." No one else in my unit could have done what he did for me. Had an officer discovered my mistake, he would have been duty-bound to report it up the chain of command. Since someone would have had to pay, that someone would have been me. Had anybody else in the unit discovered my mistake, they would not have had the spunk, self-confidence, and skill to do what Chris did. We were on the same search and destroy missions. We saw the same death and chaos. He understood. He made the decision to help me, to protect me, and then he took control of the situation and shouldered my risk.

I felt it important that Thomas know more about Chris. As our Ammo Corporal, he was responsible for supplying the entire platoon with mortar rounds and small arms. He went way beyond that. For example, once he decided we needed to celebrate Halloween. Somehow, he got a supply of balloons. Beats me how balloons would be available as a weapon, or in some way be considered contributory to the war effort, or exist in any color other than olive drab. We all painted our faces as goblins and monsters —that part wasn't too hard with our camouflage paint—and decorated our hooch with these festive balloons. Add lots of warm cans of beer from his cache, and we had a little party.

We had great difficulty with basic supplies, especially boots, which easily decayed in the jungles. To some degree, *salty*, paper-thin boots as tan as the sand were a mark of what you had seen and done, but there came a point where practicality overpowered warrior fashions. Well, Chris—MY friend—got a new pair of boots in my size for me when none were available.

I told Thomas how some of the other men were envious of Chris's position and power. His boldness served him well as he made the connections and swung the deals to serve his unit's needs. I always felt a little in awe of his abilities and confidence.

Even though I was a year older, I remember he was far more self-assured and able to shape his world as he saw fit.

I called him "Scrounger" in my book, a nickname that accurately reflected his amazing skills at securing everything we needed. He loved scooting around the base on his "mule," a small, motorized flatbed vehicle that was a predecessor to today's ATVs. If he thought he could swap something with another nearby base, like Hill 55, our Battalion Headquarters, he'd strap a few bandoliers over his shoulder and toss his M16 on top of whatever he had to trade (seems our poncho liners were worth their weight in gold), and take off with not so much as a "by your leave, sir" to anyone and then return with the materials to construct a shower for our unit—and cases of beer. In contrast, I was terrified to leave the security of our base alone.

One day, someone made a small typographical error in ordering mortar rounds for our platoon. The amount was off by a decimal point, and a small convoy of "six-by" trucks came rolling into our little fire support base with ten times the actual ammunition order. Chris took complete charge of the situation and told the drivers they had to take ninety percent of the rounds back to the main ammo depot outside of DaNang about twenty miles away. They would have nothing of it. They weren't willing to risk a second run through VC-controlled territory with that much ammo on board.

Chris organized the entire operation to accept these rounds. He was a natural decision-maker. He had most of the platoon stock every ammo bunker we had for our eight mortars while he ordered the greenest Marines to fill sandbags for new bunkers we would need. While he oversaw the construction of the new bunkers, he got on the radio with our two forward observers and told them to call in every H & I (harassment and interdiction) target they could think of. When they had returned to base, we began firing excess rounds on these targets. You would have thought a battalion of NVA was overrunning us.

Throughout the entire night, we fired round after round making the rubble bounce, pausing only to let the red-hot gun barrels cool a little. Until we were down to the number of rounds we could safely bunker, we were like a bomb just waiting for the sole rocket or enemy mortar round to send the entire base up in smoke. The next morning, we were all exhausted. It's not easy to waste the government's money.

A short time after we both had come home, I met Chris for an hour or so in Niagara Falls. Our meeting didn't go very well, I think because of me. I couldn't resurrect the camaraderie we had shared. I was so shut down emotionally that I couldn't reach out. I wasted the opportunity. Our meeting affected me. I retreated further inside and concluded, if things went so poorly with the man I cared the most about, there was no sense in connecting with any of my other fellow Marines. Better to suppress the entire experience, I thought. I didn't understand my experiences then, so I buried them under a load of shame and guilt for decades. For so many years, I squashed the experience and everything associated with it, including, unfortunately, the good people with whom I served.

"Can you tell me about Chris's death?" Thomas asked.

I explained that Chris's family discovered my book and that led to an exchange of more than twenty letters and phone conversations among Chris's family members. Then on Monday, October 28, 2002, his older brother, Hank, left me a phone message at work to call him because he felt it important to tell me something.

Before I continued, I told Thomas that I had to bring in another thread to the story to provide context. Three days before this phone message, we learned that a tragic plane crash took the lives of our beloved U.S. Senator from Minnesota, Paul Wellstone, and seven others—his wife, Sheila, their daughter, Marcia, Paul's aide, Tom Lapic, two other aides, and the two pilots of their small craft. I had met Paul and Sheila many times and, like so many others, felt them to be friends whom I greatly admired. Paul gave me a wonderful endorsement of my book, the one I am most proud of. He and I had just exchanged letters days before his death.

There was no other Minnesota politician in anyone's memory like Paul, and his death opened a giant hole here that can never be filled. It reminded me of our generation's reaction to JFK's death.

Cynthia, our friends, and I were devastated by the news, especially since it was ten days before the most crucial election in memory. This is a time when President George W. Bush and Vice President Cheney had trumped up national paranoia over Saddam Hussein and threatened a war on Iraq primarily for the purpose of solidifying national support behind war hawks and Republicans so they could take control of all three branches of the federal government, which they did accomplish ten days later. I was experiencing déjà vu while marching in the antiwar rallies and peace vigils.

Each morning began with a reloading into my attitude of an overall malaise due to the fear that the hawks on the right and the gutless Democrats would lead the US to a "pre-emptive" war for oil and world domination. Only two weeks earlier, I had the incredible opportunity to speak about politics, peace, and the pending war on Bill Moyers' national PBS program, *NOW*. The morning before the phone call from Chris's brother, I gave a speech titled, "Iraq: A Vet's View of the Next War" before a large forum at Westminster Presbyterian Church in downtown Minneapolis. On top of all of this, difficult but exciting responsibilities at work and challenging opportunities to make a real difference totally engaged my work life.

It was against this backdrop that I shut the door of my office at work that Monday morning and returned the call to Hank. "I read your book while on vacation," he said, "and I knew I had to tell you something. Chris did not die in an automobile accident." In a gentle voice that was almost a whisper, he continued. "Chris committed suicide." My suspicions confirmed, my flooding emotions cracked the dam of my resolve and leaked out my eyes.

After I settled down, I asked Hank if he thought Vietnam was a significant factor. Hank said that, in a way, his brother never left Vietnam. He said that, in spite of his tremendous accomplishments, he never felt he had done enough in Vietnam. He seemed driven to succeed in everything he tried after coming home. After getting his accounting degree and then his law degree, he worked untiringly to establish his own law firm. Later, he accepted the presidency of a major bank. According to Hank, Chris was a great father to his two boys, a loving husband, and a wonderful uncle to his goddaughter, Christine. "But when he spent the night at our house, he always asked for two extra pillows." Hank paused in his description. "I asked him why and he said he needed to put them over his ears to keep out the sounds of the exploding rounds or he couldn't get to sleep."

I wanted to know how he died, but I also sensed the telling of this dark family secret was wearing on Hank. He did tell me, though. He backed up a little on the story and explained that he had named his daughter, Christine, after Chris, and asked Chris to be her godfather. They were very close and Chris used to make the trip between his home in upstate New York to North Carolina for all of Christine's birthdays. It was on such a trip that the ghosts of Vietnam took complete control. Halfway to Hank's house for Christine's tenth birthday party, Chris stopped and pulled off the road. He emptied a can of gas into the inside of his car, tied himself to the steering wheel with his necktie, and lit a match. "They identified him through his dental records."

A long silence on the phone; my head filled with strange sounds—a tuneless humming, like muted violin strings. My stomach added growls. My body trembled and began rocking slowly. Pockets of tears greased my eyes. The phrase "death by firefight" kept rolling through my brain as I tried to absorb what my friend's older brother was telling me. We talked more, and I'm pretty sure I carried off my part of the conversation putting one word in front of another like a numbed march.

I recalled reading that some who commit suicide choose circumstances related to the primary source of their troubles. These thoughts helped me understand how Chris may have chosen his method. The most vivid memories of the cesspool that was Vietnam flared through my brain. I recalled again those horrific pictures of the Buddhist monks, beginning with Thich Quang Duc in 1963, who, in protest of South Vietnam's oppressive Diem Regime (our puppet dictator), doused themselves with gas and stoically burned to death while poised in sitting meditation. Was their chosen method of self-immolation the model for Chris? Like theirs, was his act the ultimate protest against war and oppression?

I composed myself after the conversation with Hank and called Chris's wife to let her know that I knew. She said that she was glad to hear that Hank told me because she was concerned that I was getting caught up in the family secrets. Like Hank, she confirmed that Vietnam was the source of Chris's mental problems and suicide. It was a sub-thought to his every moment, awake and asleep. She and Hank had to commit Chris to a mental hospital on two occasions, and he attempted suicide once before. Through her own choking tears, she confessed her feelings about Chris's suicide note. On top of the terrible anger at Chris for taking himself away from her and their boys, she resented him for not saying a word about her or the boys in his last letter. All fourteen pages were about Vietnam and his shame at not doing enough over there. Not one word about his post-Vietnam life, their marriage, or their two sons. She said that, in a strange way, she wanted to be more of a factor in his suicide.

For a long time afterward, the news of Chris's suicide added another layer to my already weighty grief. I began to wonder—to fear—if I still had buried memories that I was unable to face. Cynthia asked probing questions along the same theme in her loving and concerned manner. The notion that my experience, like Chris's experience, harbored the potential to lead ultimately to suicide was profoundly disturbing.

To add a period to my last sentence and the long silence that followed after I shared this story that morning in therapy, Thomas spoke up. "You mentioned the stress of your job and the factors that created such a heavy mood each morning—the pending military invasion, your presentation at the church, the loss of Senator Wellstone and others, and especially the news of your friend's suicide, but these things happened five months ago. Was there something more recent that disturbed you?"

Clamping my teeth over my words, I blurted out, "Hell yes! Bush invaded Iraq. We've started another Vietnam. Another atrocity. Another war crime."

"How does this affect you? What do you feel?"

Feelings?? Just the thought of moving beyond the protective numbness I'd used as armor for the past decades terrified me.

Going Deeper

I asked if he really wanted me to go into how this latest war affected me—the politics of it all. Thomas explained that he needed to get to know me, what motivated me, what disturbed me, and that he would not censor a topic if it is connected to my healing. So, I told him what I thought about the Iraq invasion, a little relieved to retreat into the more comfortable place of head vs. heart, of analytical thought instead of gut-wrenching emotion.

I began by explaining that I continued to have great respect for the U.S. military and especially for those who serve in it. Chris and I both had made the choice to serve in the Marines. But our military, like any tool, can be used for noble or ignoble purposes. Unfortunately for the U.S. and the rest of the world, our country has used our military might for the same reasons powerful countries have done throughout history—in pursuit of power, ego, and resources. Of course, there are exceptions, but, overall, we have used our military in service to the country's primary export—no, not democracy and freedom—capitalism. The engine of our empire is big business, and our government fuels big business with massive public subsidies, and then uses our military to provide secure markets and resources. The whole system is greased by governmental control of the masses by means of a propaganda industry—a compliant media—that runs on fear mongering. Osama Bin Laden needed the U.S. to be as 'satanic' as possible in order to mobilize and control his Islamic fundamentalists just as the U.S. needed him to control the U.S. population through fear.

Thomas interjected and tried to steer my comments more towards *feelings*, and I remember saying that every day felt like a hand reached out from the morning newspaper and slapped me with the latest example of how things kept getting worse. I theorized that when historians compose the record of the Bush Administration years later, they will be freer of the influence from the Administration's exquisite propaganda machine. Other than a few exceptions, I couldn't recall ever reading in a history book about a military action that had benign motives. I knew that veterans of the Iraq invasion and occupation will read this history decades from now and, like their fathers before them who served in Vietnam, they will know their government used and abused them just like governments have done for all time. They will be a part of the long tradition of warriors who answered their country's call to do the unnatural—to kill our fellow humans in the name of God and national self-interest.

I'm sure Thomas felt the passion in my voice. I told him that as I watched the news, I recognized those same noble patriotic sentiments on the faces of our precious young men and women we continued to send off to our country's wars. I saw the same furrows of sacrifice and worry on the faces of their loved ones that I saw on my family thirty-five years earlier. I knew that some will sacrifice limbs and some will sacrifice their lives. Others, like me, will come home having sacrificed something they didn't count on: Their idealism, their patriotism, and their faith in the motives and honesty of our leaders.

"Take a minute and breathe," Thomas advised. He unfolded his legs and let them settle to the oak flooring like they were parts of a ventriloquist's dummy. "You talked about 'crashing.' What do you mean by that?" He leaned forward shrinking that intervening space between us from comfortable to borderline intrusive.

"You know what goes on behind the sanitized shit we're fed by the media." Thomas nodded as I spoke. "Shock and Awe!" I blurted out. "Especially pretty by night, but you know what they'll find the next morning. I just couldn't take it anymore."

"What couldn't you take?

"I was tired of crying. I was tired of the feelings."

"What were you feeling?"

"I fall into a dark pit empty of everything but overwhelming sadness."

"How often?"

"Ever since coming home. It might happen every few years or many times during a difficult time." I told Thomas that, at Cynthia's urging, I decided finally to seek professional help. She called Mark, a fellow Vietnam vet whom I had helped get therapy for his PTSD. He knew the VA system.

"I will come over immediately and take you in," Mark offered. "They have a 24-hour service." I told him the next morning was early enough and he said, "You saved me, Michael. Of course, I'm going to be there for you." We talked with my voice squeaking through suppressed sobs, and Mark told me he would pick me up at 9 a.m. and walk me through the enrollment process. "I had an eighty-year-old World War Two vet do the same thing for me after you convinced me to go."

I knew my decision to ask for Mark's help instead of Cynthia's was a right decision, and Cynthia understood too. Early the next morning, he dropped everything and figuratively held my hand through the intake process at the VA. It reminded me of the sponsor role for AA members.

"Mark is a treasured friend," Thomas commented and then he slowly rose to signal the end of our session. "Jung said that a person doesn't become enlightened by imagining figures of light but by making the darkness conscious. That's what we're going to do here; make the darkness conscious. Bring it into the light."

Coming Home

"How did you feel coming home?" Thomas asked during our third session together. A seemingly simple question, but I could not give him an answer. Instead I told him the story how, when I knew the date of my release from active duty, I didn't even give my parents the courtesy of a phone call from Camp Pendleton, my stateside Marine base near San Diego. When I arrived at the Cleveland airport early one evening, I just sat down paralyzed with what I thought might be fear, but my emotions were too befuddling to determine their cause. An hour or so later, I called my older sister who was both delighted to hear my voice and as flummoxed as I was why I couldn't make the call home. Instead, she called my parents and brought me home from the airport to my family who smothered me with unconditional kisses and hugs.

"What were you afraid of?" Thomas asked. My story was the setup for this obvious question. Stuck, I still could not answer him. My eyes focused on the highly polished wood floor of his office. With a series of gentle questions, he teased out of me the memory of the fear I had that my family would not accept the person I had become; they would not forgive me for what I had done and not done in Vietnam.

"Was there something that triggered a feeling of guilt in you?" The question slapped my face and arced heat from one side to the other. It also triggered an answer to Thomas's question.

"Yes."

"Are you okay to talk about it?"

With the quivering voice and downcast eyes, I retold the mental movie that had played repeatedly in my head for thirty-three years.

Towards the end of my tour of duty, my mortar platoon rendezvoused with Charlie Company's Third Platoon at a village located in a free fire zone. Charlie Company Marines had set fire to the hooches and killed the livestock while searching for caches of food and weapons for VC or the NVA, our enemies. I vividly recalled walking past the dead body of an old man and the charred and bloated bodies of two women. This is how I described the rest of the story in my book:

A gathering of Charlie Company grunts encircled two small Vietnamese men, boys really, clad only in black shorts, blindfolded, and bound at their ankles. Lengths of thin rope cinched their hands and elbows taut behind their backs.

One of the grunts offered a cursory explanation for all gathered. "Fucking VC from that ville back there. Prisoners of war."

The prisoners had no boots, no helmets, no rifles, no flak jackets, and no mortars to protect them. They were the people we were devoting our lives to killing. They had to be the enemy. They were captured in a free-fire zone.

As he sweep-kicked the legs out from under one of the prisoners, a Charlie Company Marine growled, "That's for those land mines you bastards planted." Repeating his kick on the other prisoner, he barked a condemnation for the murder of his best friend. "That's for Becker, you asshole. For Becker."

The naming reverberated with both the reverence of a eulogy and the finality of a sentencing hearing. The two boys fell next to one another on their backs in the soft grass. They clamped their jaws and struggled to sit up.

A tension as tangible as static electricity before a summer thunderstorm crawled across my scalp. My knees wobbled, the muscles in my shoulders tensed, and the hair on the back of my neck bristled. All eyes bore down on the two of them. Another grunt fired a load of spit in the face of one of the prisoners. "Bastards!" he snarled. The prisoners' mouths and cheeks scrunched up like prunes.

I tried to conjure up a vision of some horrific evil so I could match my fellow Marines' wrath, so I could share their rage, their pleasurable revenge. So I could stomach what was happening. .... The effort provided only a momentary distraction and failed to fuel my rage. The prisoners remained kids, scared to death, actors in the surreal stage performance playing out before me.

Revenge rose to a boil around me ... Another Charlie Company Marine came close, took a deep drag on his cigarette, and dropped to one knee to gain the right angle for pressing it into the sole of the foot of one prisoner. I think the young man smelled the effect before he felt it through the thick calluses on his bare foot. It was a slow fuse to a bomb. His explosive scream marked the moment when the burn reached nerves. A scream needs no translation. It broke the resolve of the other prisoner who probably had heard about our capabilities for cruelty. The wiry muscles in his arms and legs twitched spasmodically while his nostrils flared with rapid, shallow breaths in an attempt to control his palpable terror.

From behind me, "Hard-core. Fucking hard-core."

Then a third Marine deliberately lit up a Marlboro, knelt down on the left side of the second prisoner, and buried his cigarette into the prisoner's thigh. ... No fuse this time. The young man immediately jerked away from the searing heat, reared his head back, threw his mouth fully open and pierced the air with an animal howl. [The Marine] twisted to his right and threw his full body weight across the prisoner's midsection, pinning him to the ground with his greater mass. While the young man struggled, grimacing in pain, [he] took another premeditated drag. The tip rekindled, he ground it into the prisoner's thigh at a point a little higher than the last.

A line of ants marched lock-step in the sand in front of me, responding only to the hive mentality. A giddy, out-of-body sensation freed me to float away although the interminable wails glued my boots to the soft Vietnamese soil. A bead of sweat trickled a cool line down the center of my back. My stomach grew painfully tight and my vision blurred with the turmoil of inconsistent doctrines. In an earlier life on a completely different planet, I answered at the age of thirteen what I then believed to be a divine vocation to become a Catholic priest, a saver of souls. At St. Charles Borromeo Seminary in Cleveland, I learned that Jesus taught his followers to love their enemies. Six years later, the Marines indoctrinated me to hate, to kill. The War gave me the opportunity to act out my shadow self in the name of duty and under the prophylactic excuses of "survival" and the defense, "I was merely following orders." Boot camp was supposed to inoculate me against pangs of conscience but another scream and yet another smelling salt of burning flesh made me wonder if scarring those two boys was not, in fact, what we were doing to our own souls.

I followed neither the military nor the religious doctrine. I did nothing... My own cowardice and fear of embarrassment paralyzed me. My instincts were those of sheep and lemmings. I chose silence as the course of least resistance and let the Marines burn the boys up and down their legs and chest, a dozen places each. It took a couple of minutes. It took forever.

Lt. Smith burst into the circle of consent, his barnacled face red with rage, and with an entire lung full of breath, he fired a one-word order into each of us.

"HALT!"

That is all it took. The madness of the moment halted.

However, it was not over yet. [We] gathered around

the two prisoners for pictures. ... We came together, the conquerors and the conquered. Some Marines next to me stomped the prisoners' hands and feet to the ground with their boots and others kneed them in their backs.

Standing tall directly behind the young men, I grinned for the picture. As shutters clicked, I flicked the ash of my Camel upon the black mopped head of one boy; my symbolic burning, my silent assent.[2]

My story finished, I looked up and saw Thomas, barefoot and cross-legged as usual, but with eyes pinched shut. I took two slow breaths trying to calm the sound of my beating heart that echoed in the deep stillness of the therapy room.

Finally, Thomas ended the long silence in a voice, tranquil and peaceful, "I understand. I understand fully." I never lost awareness that Thomas had also served as a Marine in Vietnam. It was only in his (and Cynthia's) nonjudging listening presence that I could be most vulnerable. "What do you feel in the retelling of your story?"

"Shame. Guilt," I confessed. "I was a coward."

No response came from Thomas as I dabbed the tears from my eyes.

"I guess I sensed that my family would somehow see that cowardice in me. My parents could always tell when I did something wrong as a kid just from looking at me. I know it doesn't make any sense, but I was just afraid to face them."

Like some toxic virus morphing in a Petri dish, the war infected my moral DNA. I came home no longer thinking with the same mind, seeing with the same eyes, hearing with the same ears. The Marines had trained me in a belief system that appealed to the still-reptilian part of my brain and empowered me to believe deep in my gut that I could kill people because they were the enemy that would be trying to kill me. I did kill people in Vietnam, some of whom had tried to kill me, but most of whom probably were civilians, just people like me caught in the carnage that is war. The first kills taught me that, but I had to keep firing for the rest of my tour of duty. I lacked the courage to stop. Sitting in that airport terminal, I was neither able to judge my actions and inactions nor to fully grasp the transformation I had undergone. All I could say was that I was totally changed. I had no time to decompress. I suffered a case of the emotional bends.

"Your soul is wounded." Thomas went on to explain. "When people suffer from moral injury, their core moral identity can be destroyed. They can develop a warped system of internal justice that demands a penance; that says they deserve punishment, to be unhappy, or even to die." Thomas leaned in even further towards me. "The Marines gave you the best training in the world to be a good soldier—even in the moral wasteland of war, but they didn't bother to undo that training to restore you as a good civilian." He leaned back in his chair. "That's why we're here together. We're going to bring you the rest of the way home."

We both took a sip a water and then Thomas restarted the train of thought. "You do know, don't you, that there was probably very little you could have done in that situation?" I shook my head. "Everyone else in that circle was either rooting for what their fellow Marines were doing to those two boys or, like you, paralyzed by the horror of it. They needed your implied consent. If you had objected and exposed their crime, they probably would have turned on you next. Only that officer had sufficient authority to stop it."

Thomas's words rang true intellectually, but they are not curative. In my heart, I know I was a coward.

Before 1996, when I began writing my Vietnam memoir, I was close-lipped about my service. Only Cynthia knew of my stories, or at least their skeletons. Somehow, Thomas took off the muzzle and my words threw their leash and took off on their own.

"What about your father? Was he in the service?"

"Marines. World War Two. He served on Guam." I remembered that my dad was the only family member to whom I dared to write anything other than vacuous letters from Vietnam. After he died, I discovered that he had saved one letter from me, the one that I recall addressing specifically to him about a month after I arrived in Vietnam. It reads, in part, "You're really the only one I could tell it 'like it is.'"

I told Thomas that I tried initially to connect with my father about my experiences after I returned home, but we both soon fell into our deep grooves of past behavior and I shut down quickly. Politics and religion—and deeper things that I would explore later on in therapy—separated us. Thomas said, "What you wanted was to be able to say to your father, 'Dad, the war was horrible,' and to have him hold you and welcome you home. But it didn't happen and it couldn't have happened given the relationships. Your father, a World War Two vet, should have said, 'I know what this is going to be like. I can help you.'"

I found it hard to express completely the differences between life in a war zone and life back in "The World," as we soldiers referred to it. During combat, my emotions became so extreme they created their polar opposites. Terror sparked adrenalized excitement. Panic birthed the resolution required to control it. The unrelenting chaos of a firefight—when I remember hugging the ground as if the safety of burrowing into it could avoid being buried in it—and finally screaming into the cacophony, "I want it to stop! I want it to stop!" led to desperation that finally neutralized these conflicting emotions and left me feeling nothing at all, floating in an undecodable world.

"In Vietnam we had a mantra—'It don't mean nothin.'" A knowing smirk showed on Thomas' face. It was a necessary, all-purpose lie we used as a bandage to keep our consciences from bleeding out and keep in the rage necessary to fight in Vietnam. We used it as a mask and blindfold to filter out the smell of burning villages and rotting corpses and screen out the faces of children drained of hope, family, and future. It hid our faces from ourselves, each other, and our role as invaders. We got so good at telling this lie that we kept telling it even after we came home to a nation that didn't want to hear our stories. We hung on to it like it was the last chopper out of Saigon.

Vietnam gave me the opportunity to explore the very best in me and to face the very worst. Bootcamp was designed to supplant the civilian ethics of us recruits with the militaristic replacements needed to deal with the barbarism that is war. There was no bootcamp to reverse-engineer the process.

When I came home, I was unaware that I was suffering from what would come to be known as PTSD, even though it formed the fault line of my personality change. I repressed the war, my experiences, and especially what I had learned about my dark side. I went back to college that fall of 1970, and tried to fit back into my former cocoon. I had to restrain my urge to revolt at the triviality of my classmates' concerns while I still had friends rotting back in the jungle, including my best friend, Chris. It strained my nerves until I thought they would fry from too much voltage. Instead of screaming, I just went along like a foreigner pretending to understand the conversation.

In Vietnam, I heard stories about anti-war protesters, and I knew my college friends thought the war was immoral, including my girlfriend at the time (not Cynthia). I gave this some weight, but I had more important matters to attend to, like checking for a trip wire one pace ahead and straining bomb crater water through my teeth. I needed a moral handhold there, illusory though it was, that we were doing something important, honorable, and necessary as I hung over the cliff of the war's dark insanity. After coming home and returning to school, I lost my voice on the highly politicized Kent State University campus. I had no tracks to press my ear to sense what was steaming my way. Fearful of the stigma society laid on Vietnam vets, I became a closet vet. I knew my handholds were slipping.

Thomas perked up and interrupted his normal serene demeanor, "You came home to Kent State? Were you there for the killings?" I told him I was there for the events that led up to the shootings but had to leave the day before the killings to catch my ship. "Ship?" Thomas blurted out. "Yeah," I started to explain.

"I joined the Merchant Marines two weeks after coming home from Vietnam and shipped out on a Great Lakes iron ore carrier. I wrote about that in my book too." Rather than letting this take us off course, Thomas said, "Just tell me the story any way you wish." He sipped from a glass of water and refolded his legs beneath him as if his knees were made of rubber.

Leo

Thomas and I then returned to the other emotions I felt upon coming home. I told him about survivor's guilt and my deep sense of remorse, that moral injury for having served in a war that society (and later myself) judged as immoral. We talked about my loneliness. I told him the story about when I paid a surprise visit soon after coming home to see Leo Heath, my good friend from high school. Like me, Leo was also a Marine grunt, only he was a machine gunner in a rifle company and had returned home six months before I did. This is how I wrote about the end of the story in my book:

> I rang the front doorbell. When the church-like chimes finished announcing me, Mrs. Heath opened the heavy wooden door. She recognized me immediately but instead of greeting me, one hand moved up slowly to cover her mouth and the other found support on the frame of the screen door that separated us. She took a deep breath, arched her eyes and brows, and choked out an anguished sob. I waited silently, paralyzed by her keening, fearful of its meaning.
>
> Recovered, but with the screen door still separating us, she began, "A few months after Leo got back, back from … Vietnam … he put a gun in his mouth … and fired. In his bedroom." The hand that covered her mouth swept across in front of her face. "Killed himself. Blood … " her words waned into fleeting images of Leo that swirled in my head; his laughs, his clowning style, his sincerity and sensitivity. He was the wise fool.
>
> "I have to go now," she said abruptly. Whatever had held her up during the months since her son's suicide just could not do it anymore. Rather than collapse as the grief stabbed at her, she slowly closed the door in my

face. She closed the heavy door on a chapter in my life, too. Still stunned, I mumbled that I was sorry, but she was no longer there to accept it. She had retreated behind the door. Its dark, carved wood sealed off all questions as effectively as Leo's thousand-yard stare. [3]

Thomas said nothing for a time after I finished the telling, then asked, "How did it feel to have two people who shared your experiences, your best friends in the war, choose suicide over dealing with pain of their lives after the war?" I told him I couldn't remember feeling much of anything after I got over the initial surprise of Leo's death. I simply moved on with my life and tried to make a living while struggling to finish my college degree. I was too driven to bother with feelings over Leo's choice. But the news of Chris's suicide thirty-three years later finally cracked my psychic shell and, like a defenseless chick, I began to peck my way out into a new world of feelings.

Fencing For Revenge

There was no boot camp to prepare us to return home from Vietnam.

Despite the numerous stories about antiwar protesters cursing and spitting on Vietnam veterans, I had no such experiences. However, there was one incident I relayed to Thomas during a therapy session about my first day back on the Kent State University campus. It was on May 2, 1970, the day before Governor James Rhodes called in the Ohio National Guard to suppress student protests of Nixon's invasion of Cambodia, a neutral country. This was two days before those same soldiers gunned down thirteen students killing four.[4]

I was visiting my former roommate and best friend, Frank, and his new roommate, Kevin, from Manhattan. I couldn't have been very pleasant to be around at the time. It was only two months after my discharge and I was jumpy and my nervousness was contagious. I felt an instant jealousy over my friend's new roommate and then a simmering rage over his opening question upon meeting me: "Did you kill women and children over there?" He delivered the line with an air of sanitized concern subtly underlain with icy sarcasm. While the veiled accusation sparked a slow burn in me, I took a deep breath, responded with an unveiled scowl, and turned back to *my* friend, Frank, with a face-saving question about his classes.

With a wry smile, I decided to tell Thomas the sequel to this little story that took place three years later in Kevin's Manhattan apartment. It involved boot camp so I knew he would be able to relate. Before I started, I reiterated that I didn't like my best friend's friend. He was much smarter than I, especially in architecture, and I had caught a bad case of halitosis of expression from the military. He played his Manhattan elitism with great skill to make me feel like a boorish hack too stupid to see that I had let myself be duped into serving in Vietnam.

During a visit to see Frank in 1973, we went over to Kevin's apartment one evening. At that time, Frank and Kevin were in architectural graduate school together at the Pratt Institute in Brooklyn. I was apprehensive as I tried to bottle old feelings of inferiority and petty jealousy.

When I noticed two foils and fencing masks in a corner of his living room, I asked Kevin if he fenced. He said he was currently taking a class, so I told him I had taken a class at Kent back in 1966. After I finished a few beers and Kevin had downed a couple of martinis, he agreed to a little sparring. His "shotgun" apartment, typical for New York City, offered a long hallway that ran from the front door and terminated in his living room. Just fine for a friendly fencing match. Midway down this hallway, we donned masks and tapped the ends of our foils together in the gentlemanly starting tradition.

Before I continued, I reminded Thomas of our boot camp training because it was an important prequel to the rest of the story. Part of every Marine's training is the fine art of bayonet fighting. With sheathed bayonets fixed to the end of our M14 rifles, we practiced for hours the parry, the thrust, and the lunge —all the same moves I had learned two years earlier in my fencing class at Kent State—plus the butt stroke, which isn't part of the fencing lexicon. I was very proud of my skills against an imaginary foe. Then we moved to pugil sticks; five-foot poles with pads at the ends the size of boxing gloves. We had mouth guards, antique football helmets, and groin guards. My opponent was several inches taller and many pounds stronger, so, like a blowfish, I tried to make myself appear larger than I really was. He had little interest in the fine points of the parry, the thrust, and the lunge. Well, he was good at the lunge. Very good. In fact, that is what he did from the instant we began the contest. No parry on my part could match his relentless attack as he pummeled me head to knee. For my every move, he had two that were faster and more aggressive. I had but one available direction, backwards. The coup de grace was a baseball bat swing to my head that spun my helmet halfway around my head and my brains with it as they led my way to the ground. I stayed down, humiliated.

Years later, I switched roles in that Brooklyn apartment. Kevin never had a chance as I swashbuckled my way right through his refined moves. With speed, agility, and an anger that powered a white-hot attack, my foil flashed like the knives of a Ginsu chef. I quickly forced him down that long hallway and right into his tastefully decorated living room where he fell backwards over his low-backed, designer couch. The curled tip of my foil dug into his chest just to the left of his breastbone. I soon left, triumphant.

I finished the story with a smug smile on my face. Telling the story served as comic relief for the otherwise dark drama of therapy work.

"OK, Michael," Thomas interjected. "That was interesting. You were not yet ready so soon after returning home to face the truths and impacts of that experience."

"Right," I said. "But everything about that guy just pissed me off."

Thomas—always the wise guru, said that I might want to view those who can push my buttons to be my best teachers. I had a sense he was right, but thought that if I had it to do over again, I would have thrusted less and parried more … just to extend the joy of the experience.

The Crash Into "Primordial Sadness"

As Cynthia describes in her book, *Shockwaves: A Practical Guide to Living with a Loved One's PTSD*: "'Unknown thought' is a term that was first coined in 1987 by psychoanalyst Christopher Bollas to describe what we know but, for a number of reasons, may not be able to consciously think yet, or that which we intuitively sense but cannot yet articulate. In other words, "[We] may know something, but don't yet know that we know it. Often, our bodies or behaviors give clues about this hidden knowledge." My unknown thoughts about the war were an ongoing, subliminal undertow on my life and body. Vietnam was like a shadowy ghost that lurked just outside the range of my peripheral vision waiting to thrust its sword between the plates of the emotional armor I had perfected. I had dammed my rising emotions with stones (*cajones*) gathered from the masculinity myths of my youth and fenced the area off with Concertina wire.

For decades after coming home I regularly exhibited the typical external manifestations of PTSD, including fear of crowded spaces, startle response, agitation, emotional numbing, intrusive thoughts, insomnia, nightmares, a feeling of impending doom, flashbacks, and hyper-vigilance (especially at night and when in wooded areas). Hyper-vigilance is like having to inhale constantly; never exhale.

I recall trying to describe to a friend what a search and destroy mission *felt* like. I asked him to take an imaginary trip the next time he was in a sauna. "Picture yourself dressed from head to toe in clothes including a heavy armored vest, boots, and a steel helmet. Now add sixty pounds of gear, ammo, and a rifle. That's about twice the normal weight for a backpacking trip. Now imagine stepping up and down off of the sauna bench to approximate the energy needed to fight your way through the thick mud and triple canopy jungles. After you've done this for two hours, take a twenty-minute rest. After a day of this, imagine digging a hole in which you will sleep for four hours and stand guard for another two. Then repeat." I paused then added, "Oh, I forgot to mention that while mosquitoes, spiders, ants, centipedes, and snakes are driving you crazy, the well-armed locals will be trying to kill you with ambushes and booby traps." I think he got the picture.

Many vets with PTSD have co-occurring addictions like alcoholism or drug abuse. Like my friend Chris, my drugs of choice were workaholism, compulsive exercise, and perfectionism. If my job didn't monopolize enough of my attention, I made sure other countless projects and commitments like triathlons and the peace the environmental movements overfilled my waking life and helped inoculate me from nightmares. Exhaustion was my sleep aide. Orderliness characterized my exterior world; one might even call it *tidy*; but it was a screen for the interior museum whose walls held a chaotic collection of pictures no one should ever have to see.

For a long time after coming home, I thought it odd that no one else dove for cover at the sound of a firecracker or other sharp noise. Most of these symptoms are much tamer now, but only recently, I realized that my hyper-vigilance habits are still just below the surface of my awareness. Invariably when I'm in a high place—be it a bridge, cliff, balcony, or tree (my son-in-law is an arborist and I have climbed numerous trees with him)—I imagine how I could survive an escape jump if forced by an attacker. When I walk, I always try to have both hands free, again, in case of an attack. I will use a backpack or briefcase with a shoulder strap rather than tie up my hands. If I must carry something, I always think how I might employ it as a decoy, shield, or weapon. To this day in restaurants, I am most comfortable only in a booth (preferably in a corner) or in a chair that is up against a wall. I chart a room, mapping out its dangers and exits.

My dentist said that I clenched my teeth at night to the point that I was fracturing them so badly he accurately predicted I would eventually need oral surgery to correct bone deterioration. He fitted me for a preventative mouth insert. My jaw muscles were so enlarged he said they looked like I pumped iron inside my mouth all night long.

A decade after finishing therapy, I had another disturbing experience. I woke up lying at the foot of our bed with both hands protecting my neck (my helmet used to protect my head). An 82 mm mortar round had exploded right outside our bedroom window. Its deafening echo banged around the inside of my head while light worms crawled over my vision after the blinding flash. I immediately leapt to the window to see the damage as I screamed at Cynthia to take cover, but no responding cry of terror came from her. Nothing. My heart pounded painfully and cold slithered up the walls of my stomach. Then I moved slowly, slowly. No sudden movements. Only shivers from my sweat-soaked T-shirt. I felt as if I might shatter into a million pieces if jarred.

Afterwards we were even able to laugh about my dream antics. I took pride that at 63, I could still perform those acrobatics without hurting myself. I was also glad that my bladder didn't fail me as it did twice in Vietnam.

The most difficult symptom I experienced since Vietnam was what I call my "crash into my primordial sadness." My sadness was a physical thing—a dark force, a looming presence, a lurking beast. With Thomas's help, I learned to recognize this deep, debilitating sadness as a psychological place with two warring inhabitants: The first is the apprehensive voice of the traumatized twenty-year-old soldier, and the other is the falsely empowered young man who takes on an attitude of contempt for his own pain. To use a male/female analogy, the timid "feminine" voice feels the pain of the trauma and the tears flow, and a moment later the harsh "masculine" voice immediately says to stuff it and quit whining. It was like those two cartoon characters of the devil and angel that sit on opposite shoulders giving opposite directions.[5]

The military (and especially the Marine Corps) promises to make men out of boys. Unfortunately, the experience usually accomplishes half the job. We come out of the fires of war with our masculine halves strong as tempered steel but our feminine halves jailed by our testosterone-driven halves. Far from the confident men they promised, many of us emerged scared *and* scarred, stuck in a sort of teenage immaturity.

My crash experience materializes as an undercurrent, like a tremor in the earth. A pit opens and I become trapped in a sketch by artist M.C. Escher of stairs that never stop going down. I become a walled off small boy. Then hammer blows of guilt, remorse, and confusion send me reeling into emotional cartwheels—feeling, stuffing, crying, rocking, being embarrassed, then berating myself; then starting all over again. I lacked the weapons to fend them off. I did not understand it; could not explain it; could not control it. My bawling like a baby so embarrassed me, I only felt safe in Cynthia's tender arms. This would go on and on until I didn't think I had any more tears left in me, and the day had gone by.

Thomas offered an explanation. "The harsh boy had served to protect you from the poison of war and to help you develop a good life. Now you are mature enough and strong enough to take the next step and re-integrate all aspects of your personality, including the tender-hearted boy." We did this extremely difficult work together, mindful that I should not use Vietnam and PTSD as a convenient excuse whenever reality did not match up to my expectations. "It's a mental disorder," said Thomas, "not a copout."

I would soon discover that therapy keeps me more honest.

2. TOWER STORIES

*My name is Charlie Porter. I was a union soldier. In '61, I signed up
to fight.*
*And it was a great adventure. But I have to tell you, not the fairy tale
I had in mind.*
And when General Lee surrendered, and victory finally arrived.
I heard no one hoot or holler. No hip-hurray for the stars and stripes.
*Back when it started, proud and foolish hearted, I thought I had a
taste for rebel blood.*
But we were only children. They killed us and we killed them.
And the misery and the dying made us numb.
*By then, holding back the sorrow, was kind of like holding back the
tide.*
I heard no one hoot or holler. No hip-hurray for the stars and stripes.
We only cried.
                    —"Charlie Porter," lyrics and music by Peter Meyer

"Michael, a lot of the combat vets I see have a particular
experience that carries a unique power," Thomas explained.
"Some call it their 'Ground Zero story.' Is that true for you?"

Immediately, my muscles began their familiar clenching
climb up my back, shoulders, and then neck and jaw. A hot
flush wrapped itself around my head to prepare for the
resolution of the fight-flight-or-freeze dilemma. Thoughts
raced towards my consciousness, "Dopplered" and intensi-
fied as they approached, then they dropped in pitch and
volume as they flew by. Equivocating, I again suggested that
Thomas could just read about my experiences in my book,
but sensed an immediate gentle push-back.

"Michael, I need to *hear* you tell your stories, not read about them."

T rapped, I knew I had to tell Thomas the tower story. A deep breath was not up to calming my racing heart. Like the soldier I was trained to be, I laid out the story in a militaristic order. Just the facts, Jack:

- Young Marine on guard duty in Guard Tower Number 2 early in his tour of duty witnessed his first casualties of war.
- Marine wasn't hurt.
- Marine wasn't responsible for harm to anyone.
- Enemy deaths only.
- End of story.

The old mantra, "It don't mean nothin" echoed in my head followed by a deep sigh of relief. But not for long.

Thomas remained stoic throughout my telling of the story until it was clear that I was done, and then he only said one word in a low but knowing voice, "Wow." We shared another long silence. Thomas sensed where my stories were going and how they truly affected me long before I finished telling them.

"Michael, I believe this is your *Ground Zero* story." My right toe began tapping out a beat that seemed to match my quivering heart.

He continued, "We need to go back up in that tower and unpack it; unpack it with great compassion." In some sense, I thought I had never come down.

"We need to slow it down and focus on the emotional connections, not just the physical things. We must become fully aware of the causes and conditions that trap you in your suffering." My teeth clenched.

"We must discover how your formative life experiences

exhibit themselves in your actions." I craved a drink of water or something stronger to tamp down the dread.

In time, I transitioned from *freeze* to resignation as I realized my eventual release from Vietnam had to be processed through that tower story.

At the end of the session, Thomas suggested I write up the tower story again but this time as I imagined it from the *ground up* instead of from the *tower down*. The following is a re-write of the tower story that blends the original as I first wrote it in *Fire in the Hole* and retell below with an imagined alternative perspective from the *ground up*, as Thomas suggested:

From The Tower Down (The Actual Story)

The thirty-foot elevation of a guard tower in Vietnam offered a long view: A view beyond the two barrack tents that housed my 81 mm mortar platoon and the platoon's four gun pits. A view beyond the bomb-cratered rice paddies that lay between our perimeter defenses and the quiet little village five hundred yards distant. A view that encompassed the entire Marine fire support base in the middle of Quang Nam Province, over one hundred miles from the Demilitarized Zone (DMZ) and half a world away from my home.

Our firebase had seven towers. From my perch in Guard Tower Number 2, I could see Guard Towers Number 3 and 1. Number 3 was to my right and southwest about seventy yards. Number 1 was about the same distance to the north and located adjacent to the camp entrance. The three towers framed the curving eastern edge of the firebase. Odd-numbered towers had two guards with an M79 grenade launcher, an M60 machine gun, and, occasionally, an M72 rocket launcher. Even-numbered towers had a lone Marine and his rifle.

I had a good view of the village and its rice fields. On that day new rice stalks, less than a foot high, painted the paddy steppes a bright pea-green color that contrasted with the iron-red of the clay paddy walls. A water buffalo pulled its plow and lone farmer through the muck of the uppermost paddy. In the village, bent old women, teeth blackened from chewing betel nuts, a few old men, and dozens of kids lived in the shanties and thatched-roof huts. It was a scene as timeless as an ancient dragonfly caught in amber. As familiar as I was with its look and rhythms, I never learned the village's name.

Able-bodied young men were conspicuously absent. No doubt they had already been conscripted by one of the three branches of the Vietnamese military: the Army of the Republic of Vietnam (ARVN), our allies; the North Vietnamese Army (NVA); or the insurgent Communist forces of the National Liberation Front, better known as Viet Cong, VC, or Victor Charlie, our enemy.

The razor-sharp edges of the double rows of spiraling concertina wire glistened in the midday sun. I had strung what seemed like miles of this stuff around our base and had the cuts to prove it. More experienced Marines had booby-trapped the perimeter wire with trip flares and Claymore mines. Each mine packed seven hundred ball bearings imbedded in a plastique shape charge designed to make literal mincemeat of intruders.

Inside the perimeter defenses and near the base's entrance and Tower Number 1, some Vietnamese from the village ran a tailor shop and a barber shop, and sold things like film, toothpaste, radios, and other black-market goods out of a rickety shack. It barely offered shelter from the sun's penetrating beam and the incessant rain of the monsoon season. In boot camp, Staff sergeant Martinez never told us Vietnamese would be on the firebases or that they would cut our hair and launder our clothes.

Kids often rummaged through our trash barrels there for food or cloth to repair the rags that hung on their little bodies. A scrap of cardboard, wood, or plastic made their ramshackle huts a little more resilient. I had never seen this degree of destitution. "Don't trust any gooks," Martinez had warned us with passionate disgust. He survived two tours of duty in Vietnam, so I had listened to him studiously.

I stepped to the rear of the guard tower and I followed the movements of my fellow Marines below. Only two things drove soldiers from the shade on one hundred-degree scorchers like this one. I chuckled as I watched the unlucky ones fill sandbags and burn shit. Empty fifty-five-gallon drums cut in half served as our septic tanks. When full, we pulled them away from the bottoms of the outhouses, added diesel fuel and toilet paper, and then stirred the twenty gallons of gumbo gingerly for a few minutes to get a smooth consistency prior to lighting it up. The ever-present odor became the signature of base camp.

Having completed a 360-degree visual reconnaissance, I rechecked my M16. Locked and loaded with eighteen rounds of high-powered ammunition with the nineteenth round already in the chamber, selector switch on SAFE, windage on the rear sight set on zero. Half out of boredom, half for the sake of perpetual practice, I swung it up and seated it deep into my right shoulder. Right elbow high, I rotated my left elbow into my rib cage and trained the sights on a rock out beyond the concertina wire. "Bone support," Martinez preached. "Be the bone equivalent of a tripod." In boot camp, he taught me to intertwine my rifle sling so tightly around my left arm and wrist I felt the weapon had grafted itself to my frame. After countless hours in painful firing positions with an empty rifle, the only reward was the repetitive dull "click" of the hammer. The consummate experience of boot camp was the rifle range. Firing live rounds at the human-shaped silhouettes on paper targets engaged all my senses and resulted in my marksmanship award. Alone in Guard Tower Number 2, I had graduated to the next stage where both the rounds and the targets were live and the reward was survival.

I squeezed off an imaginary round into the forehead of the rock, sat down on the upended ammo crate and turned my attention to *Calculus and Analytic Geometry*, by George B. Thomas Jr., the text for the correspondence course I was taking. At that time, early in my tour of duty, I still harbored the long-term view of a normal post-Vietnam world for myself.

Calculus was one of the reasons for my being in Vietnam. It was a requirement for the architecture degree I was working on at Kent State University in Ohio, but I did so poorly in it I ended up on academic probation and lost my college deferment at the end of the 1967 school year. My Cleveland draft board was about to reclassify me as "Class I-A: Registrant available for military service."

I did have choices. I could concentrate on my studies or change majors (and dreams) if necessary, to dodge or at least postpone the draft. Ironically, I did change my major after returning to school upon being discharged. Canada was also an option; ten thousand U. S. draft dodgers sought safe asylum there during the war. Or, I could stay and fight the draft and risk a prison sentence; nearly two hundred fifty thousand young American men did resist the draft laws during the War. Declaring myself a conscientious objector (CO) was not an option at the time of my enlistment. Only Quakers and Jehovah's Witnesses could get CO status because both religions had long histories of pacifism and consistent opposition to all wars. Later, CO status was available to those who could effectively argue that they weren't opposed to all wars, but only the Vietnam War. I even helped a friend draft his application in 1971 after I returned home. He was successful.

I had choices, but in the summer of 1967, I was still a patriot at heart. I was the product of the hero myths of my youth. I had absorbed the messages from my Catholic faith that condemned "godless Communists" and from the Hollywood formula movies that glorified World War Two. When President John F. Kennedy proclaimed during his Inauguration Day speech in 1961 that America would "bear any burden, meet any hardship, support any friend, and oppose any foe to assure the survival and success of liberty," I, like so many others in my generation, felt a deep stirring of romantic patriotism. "Ask not what your country can do for you, ask what you can do for your country" is still the single most memorable sentence of my life. It resonated perfectly with the altruistic ideals I learned from my church and parents. In 1965, I argued for increased U.S. involvement in Vietnam in a high school debate. That same summer, I visited the Lincoln memorial in Washington, D.C. and wept at Lincoln's eulogy to the fallen soldiers at Gettysburg, engraved on the memorial's polished white marble.

I envied the moral certitude of my parents' world that had been shaped by the "Good War." Instead of their black-and-white views, I faced an ambiguous blur of contradictory concepts, confusing events, and difficult questions: The Domino Theory; containment of Communism; treaty commitments with the nascent South Vietnamese government; searing images of the Buddhist monks immolating themselves in protest of the oppressive Diem regime, our puppet dictator; the August 1964, Tonkin Gulf incident. The political issues of the era nagged at my conscience: Was this a war of national liberation? Were we fighting on the wrong side? Was it a civil war being used as a proxy for the Cold War? Were North Vietnam and its allies waging a war of aggression? Was Ho Chi Minh a nationalist hero or a Southeast Asian Stalin? Was it wise to step in where the French left off? How could fighting, killing, and risking death be compatible with my values and dreams? How would I prefer to enter manhood: as a Vietnam vet or as a draft dodger? I lacked the conviction and courage to resist the draft and I could not shirk my duty in good conscience. Becoming a man meant becoming a soldier.

I have long hated the concept expressed by the

phrase "fuck it." It predicts a temporary suspension of reason and ethics, a personal surrender. In Nam, otherwise reasonable people said "fuck it" and opened up on automatic on any target. In the summer of 1968, I was still so angry with my father that I metaphorically gave him the finger, said, "fuck it," and joined the Marines. I figured I would teach him a lesson if I went and got myself killed in Vietnam.

The Marines promised to make a man out of me and offered the shortest time in uniform—eighteen months of active duty. The thought of the GI Bill to help finance school after the service sounded very good. I was having a hard time working my way through college. The mindless job in the military of simply taking orders looked a lot easier than succeeding in architecture school.

I shaved my head the night before I shipped out for six months of training: Boot camp at Parris Island, South Carolina; Advanced Infantry Training School and Mortar School at Camp Geiger in Charlotte, North Carolina; and final training in Camp Pendleton near Oceanside, California. By March 1969, I was in excellent physical shape, trained to kill and willing to die for my country. Then my Commander in Chief, President Richard M. Nixon, sent me to Vietnam to put my new skills and sense of purpose to the test.

Back in Guard Tower Number 2, the text on my lap beckoned: Calculus, the study of change and motion. As I had done at Kent State just months earlier, I again struggled to calculate the distance between two points via a series of estimates of the halfway point. The more numerous the estimates, the greater the precision. Even though the dichotomy of mathematics' exactness was in stark contrast to the War's uncertainties, the calculus technique of getting from point A to B by multiple halfway measures seemed ironically consonant with the series of decisions I made, each bringing me halfway to where I was sitting at that moment.

My mind wandered again and so did my gaze. About thirty yards directly to the west, I noticed two boys rummaging through a garbage can located next to one of Charlie Company's barrack tents. It was unusual for Vietnamese to wander this far from their shack by the base entrance. The boys looked about eight and ten years old. They were both frail and emaciated. Our garbage was their feast.

From The Ground Up (My Imagined Story And Characters)

The mother could postpone no longer. She called her two sons to her side to give them instructions for their future; a future she may never witness. At ten, Le was two years older than his brother whom everyone called Chuot, his nickname, which means *mouse*. "Sit," she told them, "and listen very carefully. This is important."

The dying glow from the cooking fire gave flickering form to her weathered face as they sat cross-legged on their rice mats in the small family house. With whispered tones that signaled both gravity and anxiety, she began. "Your father has a task for you, but you cannot speak one word of it to another person. Not one word. Do you understand?" The two boys promised to be silent. "You will travel tonight with your Aunt Dieu to the Han Song village and stay there for several days. You will do exactly as she tells you. Her friend Lan has a shop on an American military base where she gives haircuts to the American soldiers and washes their clothes. She will show you how to collect things from the garbage cans there."

"But why, Mama?" Mouse's patience was limited.

"Hush, little Mouse. I will tell you. Your father is doing his duty for his country, is he not?" Both boys nodded. "Your uncles are also fighting with the brave People's Liberation Army Forces to defeat the American invaders and the Vietnamese traitors who are their friends. Before the PLAF, your ancestors defeated the French and Japanese colonizers, and before them the Chinese invaders. For hundreds of years, we have been fighting people who have wanted to take over our country. Now it is your turn. Do you understand?" the older brother, Le, answered "yes," but with false bravado.

"But what must we do, Mama?" asked Mouse. "Collect garbage?"

"At first, yes, you will collect garbage. But after the Americans are used to seeing you, you will leave them something; something that will send the message that they should not side with our country's traitors in our civil war. You will show them that they are not safe here, even on their own bases." She paused and took a deep breath. "You will plant a bomb that will tell the Americans that we will fight them to our last soldier, to our last breath if necessary, just as President Ho has asked of us."

Again, it was Mouse who interrupted with a voice as tiny as his body. "But why us, Mama? Why not somebody else?"

"Your father asks this of you because his commander requested it. You are just the right age to make it work. It will work. Your Aunt Dieu and her friend will make sure that you will be fine. I promise." The certainty in her assuring words was not structurally sound; supported more by hope and prayer than fact. "The bomb will not go off until after you leave the base and are safe. You will be home that very night. Your father will be proud of you."

The stillness of the darkening night and waning fire cloaked the three small figures in a pact that had the potential to further the eventual defeat of the world's most powerful military force.

"We haven't much time. Dress in your work clothes. The

worse you look, the more invisible you'll be. They already think we are lower than dogs, so if you look as hungry and poor as one, they'll feel sorry for you and not bother you. If they talk to you, say this: 'Marine, number one.' They like that." She didn't want to tell them too much. She knew they'd get all the instructions they needed when the time came. "Take only what you can carry in your rice bag. Now go and get ready. Your aunt will be here very soon. Le, help your little brother."

She could have told them sooner. Her husband told her what was required several days earlier, but she couldn't bear to have her sons share her anxiety. The thought of them leaving sucked at her soul like paddy muck. She must be strong, she thought to herself. Strong for her husband. His commander said the PLAF would pay the family. Her husband's pay, when it came, could not even pay for basic necessities. The war prevented normal farming. It was only the help from her sister's family that kept them from going over the brink into starvation. Although her husband never said anything explicitly, she knew that there would be consequences if they refused. Strong as she was, she could not hold back the quaking sobs and words that silently escaped her pursed lips. "My boys. My boys. My boys."

Le and Mouse's Aunt Dieu escorted the boys on the three-hour walk to Han Song village, which is located near Da Nang in northern Quang Nam Province. She left them at her friend's house and returned home that same night. Late the next day, the boys met the friend, Lan, after she had returned from a long day at the little shack she operated just inside the perimeter of Concertina wire on the nearby Marine Fire Support Base Puller.

At daybreak the next morning, Lan and the two boys walked the mile to the guard shack at the base entrance as Lan gave them instructions for the day. Before they had left, she had slipped an oversized transistor radio into Le's rice bag. When the guard emerged from the shade of the shack, Mouse took a half step back. He had never seen such a tall man nor one with red hair and such a red face. The guard towered over him with heavy boots, body armor and helmet, and a strange weapon that looked small compared to his tall but lean body.

When the Marine shifted his glare at the two grimy boys dressed in rags, Mouse's fascination with the man was instantly replaced by a rush of heat that rose into his little head and turned it almost as red as the guard's. "What-the-fuck's with these gook kids?" Mouse tipped his head down so the brim of his conical hat hid his downcast eyes and dry quivering lips.

"They help me," was all Lan had to say about them as she turned over identity papers for herself and the two boys. The guard gave a cursory look at their papers and roughly searched the two baskets holding cleaned and pressed Marine fatigues that hung from her shoulder pole.

This was the only part of his job that the red-haired guard loved. Bullied back home as a kid; here, he was a god who, even at 150 pounds, could lord over this little woman and these scared children. With his rifle as scepter, he held their futures in his hands.

"Hey little gook. Whaddya' got in the bag," the guard asked Le. When he saw the radio, he added another insult. "Bet that piece of shit only plays fucking gook music. Number 10. I better not hear it. I hate that shit."

"Go," he said with a twist of his head. "Didi mau!" he ordered as the three of them walked through the wire and past the other guard who slept through the entire scene with his arms on the window ledge right next to the loaded breech of the M60 machine gun. It was only a hundred feet to the "gook shack," as the Marines called it. Two Marines were already waiting with their dirty laundry and the need for a high-and-tight haircut.

A little later, with the radio softly playing rock music on AFVN, both boys walked slowly with their shoulder bags to the closest garbage can right under the shadow of the Guard Tower Number 1. Thirty feet above them, two Marines armed with an M79 grenade launcher and an M60 machine gun kept a constant watch of the base perimeter. The boys made a show of rummaging through the garbage and added cans and some discarded clothing to their bags, just as Lan had instructed. At the next can, Le tucked a crumpled C-ration carton under his arm to make the garbage collection ruse more complete. No one said a word to them. The machine gun drumming of their little hearts subsided. Maybe they were invisible like their mother had predicted.

Lan had told them to find a garbage can that was close to one of the large canvas tents the Marines used as barracks, but both of the cans they had visited were on the edge of the perimeter road and in the open. Then Le spotted a can that was right next to a barracks tent, but it was as far away as a paddy dike was long. Too far to risk it, Le decided, so they returned to the shack and helped Lan for the rest of the day. The second day was a repeat of the first. Lan decided that the distant can was the goal for the third day.

That night, Lan called the two boys to her and brought in the transistor radio. She removed its front and revealed its gutted interior with two pounds of C-4 plastique explosive molded into the cavity. With whispered words, she showed them the pen-sized detonator that was wired to the radio's battery housing and then to a cheap watch that was stuffed into a corner. The watch had its bezel and hour hand removed. Lan explained that when the minute hand touched a small metal post that had been welded to the top of the watch face, the electrical circuit was completed. She set the watch for five minutes after the hour but did not start it by winding. "We'll wind the watch tomorrow morning and add the batteries before we go to the base. Le, you will place it in that far garbage can you told me about and you both will walk back to the shack and then off the base with me. You will walk. Understand?" Both boys nodded reflexively but Mouse only understood that it was his older brother's responsibility.

The boys had talked about such bombs with their friends but had never seen one before. Scores of times they scrambled for safety in the family's underground shelter as the armies fought each other in this three-sided civil war. Now they were soldiers just like the generations before them. Somehow, they needed to muster the courage to hand-carry this bomb to the invaders. The challenge alone aged them both, but it was insufficient to stop the bile from scouring Le's throat.

"Papers," the guard demanded. He was new; not the regular guard with the red hair who had been paying little attention to the three Vietnamese civilians on the prior two mornings. While he called on the landline to headquarters, small rivulets of sweat cut cool channels of tension down Le's back. In his bag was a small ticking watch and enough explosives to destroy everything within a ten-foot radius. Minutes crawled by at the pace of the sun's winking ascension in the morning sky. Finally, the guard let them through. Not knowing how much time they had left, Le and Mouse walked a little more quickly to the first two cans on their now-regular garbage collection route. To Le, the third can appeared at the end of a long hazy tunnel that led into the very bowels of the enemy's camp.

The fight-or-flight response, which operated automatically at the cellular level at the ages of the boys, is not a simple fork-in-the-road type decision that ends there. Incessantly, they had to decide against retreat and to rein in the sprint their legs craved.

When they reached the distant garbage can, Mouse stayed close to help shield Le from view as he slipped the radio into it just as they had practiced it countless times over the prior two days. The garbage can was empty and the sound of the heavy bomb hitting the bottom three feet away resonated like a base drum—or an explosion. It was just too much for Mouse. With the smell of his own urine filling his flared nostrils, he started back at a jog even as his older brother fired a lungful of whispered air, "Walk!"

"Hey! What are you dinky dau gooks doing?" demanded a Marine from the doorway of a nearby hooch. The bellowed question, barely audible over the boys' heartbeats, panicked them both into full *flight* mode and, at a full run, Le quickly outpaced his younger brother. Four, maybe five seconds later, a crunching, bone-crushing explosion with garbage can shrapnel and hot gasses moving out at nearly five miles a second shredded the adjacent barrack tent, instantly killed two Marines, and severely wounded several more. The shock wave knocked the two boys to the ground. With volcanic adrenaline propelling them on their escape mission, they were back on their feet madly running again, numbed to the blood that oozed from their now-deaf ears and the silent explosions that ricocheted around the insides of their skulls.

From The Tower Down (The Actual Story Continues)

Instinctively, I traded tools, dropped *Calculus and Analytic Geometry,* and grabbed the pistol grip of my M16 while assuming the standing firing position. I thumbed the selector off SAFE, past SEMI and all the way over to AUTO as I shouldered the weapon, oblivious as to whether the target was another paper silhouette from the rifle range or a young boy.

Ignoring the bitter taste of adrenaline, the constant drills by Staff sergeant Martinez came alive in my head. "Snap in. Aim in. Breath control. Focus on the front sight post, not the target." Only on the rifle range did the drill Instructor ever use a soothing voice. His coaching was as meditative as a Zen centering exercise. "Keep it to three-round bursts. The up-and-left pull of the M16 will waste the Marine Corps' fourth round." Through the circular rear sight, I saw the target do a running dance between the front sight post and the left edge of the front sight as I led him. I recalled the firing range adage: aim low when firing down. My chest muscles had already halted their bellows action. "If you're squeezing that trigger oh so slowly," advised Martinez, "you won't know when the hammer is released. Learn to make that moment happen between your heartbeats or you'll never get off my rifle range." His relentless training had set me on the same automatic fire as my weapon.

A three-round burst erupted from the machine gun to my north in Tower Number 1. The gunner had a clear shot at less than twenty yards of the two boys as they ran directly toward him. The fine dust danced a three-step toward the taller and faster boy. The next burst ripped through his right thigh, belly, and chest and sent him reeling. An instant later, after a minute adjustment by the gunner, three more lead slugs, rocketing at Mach 3, bore clean through the chest of the smaller trailing boy. He collapsed abruptly in a heap not more than three feet from the other boy. Then I heard the heavy metallic, jack hammer sounds from the other machine gunner in Tower Number 3. A moment later, came the higher-pitched reports of M16 fire, and the small area around the boys became a free-fire zone.

In boot camp, Staff sergeant Martinez described in detail how the 5.56 mm M16 round was designed to be just enough off-balance so it would tumble after entering soft flesh. I had studied the complex trajectory of an imbalanced object as a practical example in my calculus course. In the textbook case, it was a tossed hammer. Now I was observing this equation in terms of hot metal tossed through little boys.

The two boys came apart in the firing frenzy. Sound reverberated from all directions for an interminable time as the metal opened them up, exploded their faces, and spilled their intestines onto the reddening sand. They no longer looked human, more like freeway road kill when the evisceration is so severe you cannot identify the species. I stared, but could not fire. Targets no longer, I saw only dead children.

From The Ground Up (My Imagined Story Continues)

In the confusion that immediately followed the explosion, Aunt Dieu's friend, Lan, saw it all and slowly walked the short distance to the front gate holding her stomach and gagging. With a hidden finger down her throat, she was able to vomit at the feet of the same guard that had let her in less than an hour earlier. He was happy to let this disgustingly sick woman leave while he prepared for an attack from beyond the base's defenses. Within twenty-four hours, she was well on her way to North Vietnam via Cambodia on the Ho Chi Minh Trail.

Two weeks later, soldiers of the Army of the Republic of Vietnam, led by a tall U.S. Marine, forced the village leaders to turn over for questioning, the mother of two boys suspected of being responsible for a terrorist bombing at Fire Support Base Puller. Le and Mouse's mother was taken to the Combined Military Interrogation Center and was never heard from again.

From The Tower Down (The Actual Story Concludes)

I do not remember what happened to the boys' bodies. I do not remember what happened to the Charlie Company Marines who were resting in the hooch before the explosion. I vaguely remember hearing low moans and cries for a medic, seeing blackened and bleeding bodies. A medevac chopper probably arrived within minutes to whisk them to a hospital ship moored in the South China Sea, but I cannot be sure.

I do remember wondering how parents could send their children on a suicide mission. I admired the intensity of their dedication if not their methods. Their mission succeeded. Days later, we learned that two of the wounded Marines had died. I realized the Vietnamese were fighting for their land, for their next meal, for their lives. For them, war was a life-long, inter-generational, noble endeavor. For me, the War had become little more than a job. I had joined it with confused motives that included both patriotic duty and a subconscious need for a male rite of passage. Two dead boys—the first of many deaths I would witness during my tour of duty—taught me what was at stake.

The incident with the two boys was easier for me to live with because I did not pull my trigger. Others did the killing. But this I know: if the incident had occurred just one month later after I had experienced my first search and destroy missions and patrols to find the bodies destroyed by my mortar rounds, my bullets would have been the first to rip the boys to shreds. Although I did not pull my trigger then, their two faces are among so many others that haunted my dreams.

I never picked up that calculus book again.

After sharing the *actual* tower story with Thomas, he explained that physical wounds of war and violence, although significant, are often less traumatic than psychic wounds. "You can treat physical wounds," he said. "You can manage them and people can see and acknowledge them." Sitting Buddha-like in his 60s-style office chair, Thomas spoke with a quiet energy that resembled a hydro plant's resonating electric hum (or ohm?). "Moral injury wounds the spirit. It can't be seen as clearly or treated as easily. The young Marine who went up in that tower was not the same one who came down. When he saw the shattering of the two little boys, his world shattered as well."

Going "back up into that tower" became the metaphor Thomas returned to repeatedly when it was time to "unpack" an emotional issue. Together, we explored how the war (and later my childhood experiences) contained the seeds of my suffering. I learned to slow down the mental video version of each story and see how it interconnected with my past and was much more complex than I realized. By acknowledging how my Vietnam experiences affected me as a twenty-year-old, I began to draw out the poison of war. I looked deeply into the nature of myself to plumb the depths of my suffering. While so many others advised me to forget the past and move on, I learned that hiding or avoiding does not eliminate suffering; it just drives it deeper where it can control us more profoundly. Thomas helped me expose my anger, embarrassment, guilt, shame, and confusion so that I could no longer deny my suffering; so that I could swim in it instead of being drowned by it. He invited me to live with my emotions without judgment. "Emotions are neither right nor wrong," he explained, "neither good nor bad. They simply are."

Becoming more aware, more *mindful*, didn't translate directly to peace. Life became clearer, even simpler and much more genuine. But not easier. Society teaches us that suffering is an enemy that we should avoid. Why invite in what is unpleasant, disappointing, or difficult? We prefer quick fixes. Got a headache? Take a pill. Painful memory? Get over it. But the hard truth is that life *is* suffering. Thomas said that it is only through a relationship with my pain and sadness that I can reach the other side. "Only then can you know and touch the opposite—your pleasure, your joy, and your happiness." At first, his comments were like Rorschach inkblots; seemingly undecipherable without an instruction manual. The process to fully realize the validity of his approach took nine months of hard work; the same time as the average gestation period for human beings. By the end, I gave birth to a more complete and genuine self.

With Thomas's help, I was able to invite my whole self into my life, to integrate all the different parts of myself into one whole, and to participate more fully in my life.

PART II

Why I Went to Vietnam

Prelude: Prayerful Pilgrims

The windshield wipers were the metronomes of my mood. Theirs was a slow and even beat; reliable, dependable, and unwavering. They cleared a view through the chaos of weather that beat at the car's windshield. On the other side of the streaked glass, the world whipped turbulent waves of uncertainty. Wind, rain, darkness, cold. The wipers dragged the beams of oncoming headlights in an arc across the Safety-Glass protection. As steady as his hand on the wheel was the drone of my dad's voice, "Our Father who art in Heaven, hallowed be Thy name. ..." The boat-like suspension of the brand new, 1966 Ford Country Squire station wagon steered a hushed smooth course through the torrent as we sped eastward between downtown Cleveland and Lake Erie at fifty miles per hour on the city's first freeway.

"Thy kingdom come, ..."

The rosary is a rhythm song; a cadence sung in monotone. Our little choir—my mom, dad, and me—performed the mantra with a well-practiced diligence. We breathed in at the same moments between the phrases. My mind tried to rediscover the freshness of the words, but countless repetitions had long since eroded their meanings. "Give us this day our daily bread..." As a child, I thought that was where food came from; directly from God. "And forgive us our trespasses as we forgive those who trespass against us." This sentence did occasionally give me pause. It had substance and a formula.

The wipers were the maestro's baton syncopating each phrase and each unison breath.

Peace.

We could have been the subjects of a Norman Rockwell painting. He might have titled it "Prayerful Pilgrims," because pilgrims we were. My father, a very successful entrepreneur who worked impossible hours seven days a week as I grew up, was also on a holy mission as a soldier of his Lord. Over the next thirty years, his pilgrimage would ultimately demand the sacrifice of his vision and blind him to the visions of others. Seeking the "Miracle of the Sun" many years after that rainy night's drive, the laser intensity of the noonday sun over the Medjugorje shrine in the former Yugoslavia helped to deteriorate the retinas of his intense blue eyes as his devotion seared his soul with a tunnel-vision purpose to proselytize.

Born of a dirt-poor, Mississippi farm family, Mom took refuge from his fanaticism in the bottle of vodka she kept hidden in the kitchen cabinet, or by drinking in all the love her seven children could pour out to her. Her lifelong sacrifice, constant work for and dedication to her family, infectious laughter, and her intelligent and razor sharp wit throughout it all earned her a reverential martyr status, which was further enhanced by her stoic endurance of chronic arthritic pain that sparked a tortuous wince for so many of her later years.

Until I became a father myself (and then a grandfather), I could never fully comprehend her devastation after the death of her twenty-one-year-old son ten years after that rainy night's drive. Her grief paralyzed her as she sequestered herself in her bedroom for two months afterwards. I always felt she settled for the unhappiness of the life she knew rather than face the uncertainty of a different future. Even though premature graying completely silvered her full head of wavy hair, it only matured her movie star looks and fine sculpted cheeks and nose.

The pilgrimage of the car's seventeen-year old passenger was soon to shift into high gear in a drastically different direction.

"And lead us not into temptation, but deliver us from

evil. Amen." I had no clue about evil, real evil. In fourth grade, Sister Margaret tried to drum in the idea that the Devil was the source of all evil. That was certainly more convenient than what I experienced just three years after that car ride. In a jungle on the other side of the world, I gave passive assent to the physical abuse of two boys at the hands of this country's mighty military. I never saw the Devil in Vietnam, but I did see in the eyes of my fellow Marines revenge, racism, and even pleasure while inflicting severe pain on the defenseless, and I saw my own moral cowardice.

The rain had ceased, but the tall oaks that arched over the long curving drive onto the campus of Borromeo High School Seminary continued to drip through the misty glow of the streetlights. It was a comforting scene that welcomed me back to this hallowed institution for the Catholic priesthood after the spring break visit with my family near the end of my senior year. Echoing an ancient tradition, the carillons from the chapel's bell tower rang out the reminder that Grand Silence would begin in exactly one hour. After nearly four years, the sound of the bell alone was sufficient to trigger the meditative calm that accompanied the ten-hour silence that nestled us each night.

This was the difficult time between homes. I returned Dad's firm handshake and thanked him for the ride back to school. Handsome and still trim at fifty with only slight graying at the temples of his full head of jet-black hair, he replied, "Work hard, Son," and then walked back to the car. The sallow parking lot lights softened the colors of his dapper, tweed sport-coat and tan pants while his black-and-white wing tips tapped out his departing steps on the wet concrete. Even though they had made the hour's drive to and from here many times, I could feel Mom's reluctance to say goodbye as she gave me a tight hug and a long kiss on the cheek.

A slight breeze knocked a few drips down on us from the wet leaves overhead, or perhaps it was Mom's tears. She turned quickly to leave. Her ankle-length gabardine raincoat made her appear a little taller, reminiscent of Ingrid Bergman in *Casablanca*.

I grabbed the leather strap on the aluminum case that bulged with the clothes she had so carefully cleaned, ironed, and folded for me, and headed towards my dormitory, Archbishop Hoban Hall. I had to help oversee the return of the thirty freshmen that five other seniors and I mentored there, and I was running late. After a few steps, I turned; half expecting to see my mother still standing stoically, but saw instead the tail-lights of the Country Squire disappear into the tunnel of oaks.

Long before all my friends and I were done trading stories of our adventures over the weeklong vacation, the Vespers bell signaled the start of Grand Silence and Evening Prayers. Stories ended in mid-sentence, and we all began the peaceful processional towards the chapel. We had said goodbye to the outside world and our families, and returned to a voluntary discipline in preparation for a life devoted to our religion and the service of others. We were teenaged pilgrims in search of sacred inner peace and strength of character.

Father McLaughlin began the service that was to be one of the last for me at Borromeo Seminary. With symbolic extravagance, he burned expensive incense. Its calming perfume enveloped us like a Lake Erie fog while the soft arpeggios of a somber Bach sonata reached high for the candle-lit arches. Father McLaughlin knew the importance of engaging all the senses to help us rekindle our vocations after our time away from our cloistered refuge. To resume the treasured journey inward, we chanted. We meditated. We prayed. "Our Father who art in Heaven, hallowed be Thy name, ..."

3. FAMILY, CHURCH, AND RAGING HORMONES

I believe in Spinoza's God who reveals Himself in the orderly harmony of what exists, not in a God who concerns himself with fates and actions of human beings.

—Albert Einstein

By my reckoning, the more or less solidly reality-based [Americans] are a minority, maybe a third of us but almost certainly fewer than half. Only a third of us, for instance, believe with some certainty that CO_2 emissions from cars and factories are the main cause of Earth's warming. Only a third are sure the tale of creation in Genesis isn't a literal, factual account. Only a third strongly disbelieve in telepathy and ghosts.

Two thirds of Americans believe that 'angels and demons are active in the world.' At least half are absolutely certain *Heaven exists, ruled over by personal God—not some vague force or universal spirit but a* guy. ...

A quarter believe vaccines cause autism and that Donald Trump won the popular vote in the 2016 election. A quarter believe our previous president was (or is) the Antichrist. A quarter believe in witches. Remarkably, no more than one in five Americans believe the Bible consists mainly of legends and fables—around the same number who believe that 'the media or the government adds secret mind-controlling technology to television broadcast signals' and that U.S.

officials were complicit in the 9/11 attacks."
—Kurt Anderson,
Fantasyland: How America Went Haywire, A 500-Year History

"Are you alright, Michael?" Thomas leaned forward and his eyes narrowed in intensity. We had just finished another grueling session of going "back up into that tower" to unearth feelings the "harsh boy" in me had entombed for thirty-four years.

A well-practiced "Yeah, I'm fine" automatically came out of my mouth while my mind recognized it as a lie.

Thomas tacked to what I presume he thought would be a relief via a topic less likely to dredge up mucky emotions. "Can you tell me some of the reasons you decided to enlist in the Marines?"

E very Tuesday morning for nine months I made my way to Thomas's office, and we examined how the effects of Vietnam entangled my life like jungle vines. Unlike his questions about my feelings, which I found utterly befuddling, the question of why I enlisted was about history. This I could do, and I savored the chance to explain something I understood. This is the history I summarized for him:

Two years after high school graduation from the womb-like serenity of the Catholic seminary, I joined the Marines, fully aware in 1968 that the decision would likely send me to Vietnam. Everyone thought I was crazy to enlist; my family, friends, my girlfriend back then—especially my girlfriend. They could have been speaking Swahili, because the only language I understood came from an inner voice that I could not translate until many years after returning home. When I joined up, there was only one person I knew in the service, Leo, my good friend from high school. I now fully understand my reasons for enlisting, and, with the practiced precision of my rational education, I've categorized them into five neat little boxes, although they do tend to fight this corralling. They are similar to those I have heard from the scores of vets I have talked with over the years.

Family And Church

My parents raised me with the typical values of a middle-class, suburban family in the 1950s. The near-mythic struggles of the Great Depression and World War Two honed their vision. My mother grew up in a large, farm family from Mississippi. She said she joined the WAVES (Women Accepted for Volunteer Emergency Service—a division of the U.S. Navy), "to get out of town and meet some men." She served in Washington D.C. as a *degarbler*, a code breaker, and spoke with great pride about how her unit cracked a critical Japanese naval code during World War Two. As for my dad, he loved to repeat wonderfully romantic stories about being an orchestra leader in the Marines and later running the Enlisted Men's Club called the "Slop Chute" on Guam soon after the Marines captured the island from the Japanese. He was fond of saying, "I guess I went through the war with a beer in one hand and a baton in the other helping the fighting men fight."

My dad told me that Mom was the most beautiful woman he'd ever met. The wedding picture that graces our fireplace mantel shows they could have been stand-ins for a 1940s movie poster.

After my mother converted from the Methodist faith, they were both devout Catholics who instilled in their children a very strong work ethic and, in concert with our church and Catholic education, a solid sense of patriotism.

Dad was a very successful entrepreneur who worked seven days a week. After my older sister and I were born, he and Mom practiced the only birth control method allowed by the Catholic Church, the rhythm method. As evidenced by my six siblings, they must have practiced a lot in what Mom once called their bedroom "playpen." Amazingly, Mom had two or three babies in cloth diapers at all times during a fourteen-year period. In addition, she kept a spotless house; did all of the cooking, shopping, laundry, and ironing; and worked evenings for the family business long into the night.

At age thirteen, Jesus "spoke" to me and said I had the divine gift of a vocation to the priesthood. Against the urging of everyone in my family (including my devoutly Catholic father), I left home after grade school to attend boarding school at Borromeo Seminary on the east side of Cleveland. Since that September day in 1962, I never spent more time than a few weeks at home, with one three-month exception before I went into the service. The seminary was a wonderful, life-shaping experience for me. I lived my Catholic faith—fully integrated in body, mind, and spirit. It still stands as one of the happiest periods of my life. Plus, being on the path towards the priesthood gave me very special status in my family. When I came home for a short visit, my family treated me like royalty. One of my brothers would begrudgingly give up his bed for me, Mom would cook my favorite meals, and Dad would ask how my studies were going. I was hot stuff. As time passed, my parents looked more positively on my decision to attend Borromeo. I was my parents' ticket to Heaven considering the highest achievement for Catholic parents was to raise a son to be a priest.

Place shapes us. I learned to love meditating in the silent sanctuary of the seminary chapel. Its stillness was tactile; just like a breeze giving soul to a deep canyon. Silence absorbs the trivial. I imagined the chapel's columns channeling the river of my thoughts and prayers heavenwards.

The seminary was where my history teacher, Father Wysinski, pulled back the curtain and let me see how the early Church fathers pushed the levers and buttons to establish the Church's dogmas. When we discussed the contradictions between the Old and New Testaments, Father Wysinski told me the Old Testament was metaphorical and not to be taken literally. The New Testament was the foundational text for the Catholic Church. When we discussed the inconsistencies in the New Testament, Father Wysinski said parts were metaphorical and not to be taken literally; the Church teachings were the heart of the

Church. We learned about the Holocaust, and the antisemitism of the New Testament and the Church's teachings. That's when Father Wysinski talked about the Popes who fathered children and the time when there were two and even three competing Popes at once. I learned about the great Church councils, like Nicaea and Trent, convened to deal with heresies, contradictory beliefs, and schisms. Father Wysinski set up his Church history lesson so well I expected a description of a miraculous answer directly from the mouth of God to the Pope. My expectations were dashed, however, when he said, "the Cardinals voted on it." Dogma by democracy?

I realized the stone markers for my spiritual path were anchored in shifting sand. For the first time, I began to see my religion as more a human creation than the divine one I had been led to believe since early childhood. My seminary teachers gave me the analytical tools and the history lessons to outgrow my childhood faith. Dogma began to morph into myth and legend.

Prior to the seminary, my parents and the Catholic Church had drilled into me divinely determined absolutes. Angels hovered over me like drones ready to fire a Hellfire missile the instant I strayed. The rules directed the path of my belief. [6]

No Atheists In A Foxhole

I distinctly remember having a lengthy discussion about Catholicism near the end of my tour of duty in Vietnam with my best friend, *Scrounger*. We were on guard duty one night in a squat, sandbagged bunker that was built into the perimeter berm of our remote fire support base. The norm was for two men to serve a solitary four-hour watch while the other man rested. I pulled the 10-to-2 am slot. Sleepless in Vietnam's stifling heat, Scrounger decided to join me, so we agreed to share both watches all night long. I reimagined that night and reconstructed the conversation (Scrounger gave me my nickname, "J.M."):

"You're Catholic, right, Scrounger?"

"Yeah, J.M. Why?"

"Well, I was raised Catholic too, and I was thinking about all the stuff they crammed into us as kids—you know, the priests and nuns."

"You still Catholic?" he asked.

"That's what's stamped on my dog tags." I fingered one of the two silvery IDs that dangled from my neck as if I could read the word in Braille on this moonless night. Scrounger didn't pressure me for a more specific answer. By that time, I no longer accepted most Catholic beliefs, but I was not comfortable going public with the notion of having rejected Christianity too. With an invitational lilt to my voice, I continued, "Some of it *is* pretty crazy. What do you remember?"

"Lots," he said as he warmed to the night's discussion topic.

"Cigar?" he asked as he extended a thin package that held

four cigarillos. Scrounger and I shared the same body type, lanky stretched over an average height. But nearly a year of sweating in Vietnam's sauna wilted our normal 165 pounds down to sub-130. I took a cigar hoping smoking it would advance a badass Marine image. It was a Swisher Sweets, which, ironically, conveyed an undersized phallic message.

We took turns ducking into a dark corner of the bunker to light up. I retrieved a bottle of the liquid amphetamine, Obesitrol, I had bought from the Vietnamese tailor on the base and downed a dollop and passed it to Scrounger. "Take a bite." Its cough-syrup sweetness left a metallic aftertaste. Unlike the many reports of heavy drug use in Nam, alcohol and pot were the only other drugs my unit used as far as I knew, and only when off duty within the relative safety of the fire support base.

With a theatrical monotone voice in between hits on the stimulant, Scrounger surprised me by reciting a lesson from the little blue booklet that anchored our childhood faith, the *New Baltimore Catechism*. It was our cultural touchstone. "There is only one God, and three Persons in that God: Father, Son, and Holy Ghost."

"Excellent, my man." I chimed in. "Okay, my turn. 'Jesus, the Son of God, was both God and human. He died on the cross to atone for *our* sins.'" Before I yielded the floor, I added, "The Jews killed Jesus," then, with a twist of sarcasm, "*Not* the *Italians*." We both chuckled over the obvious antisemitism of our common upbringing.

"OK, J.M., check this one out," Scrounger said through a cupped drag on his perfumed cigar. "The only way to God and Heaven is through Jesus." Did a smoke ring just form above his head or was it just trick of battle fatigue mixed with the speed?

"The best way to Jesus is through His mother, the

Blessed Virgin Mary," I countered.

"The only way to God and Jesus and Mary is through the Holy Mother the Church."

"Touché." Before he could launch his next dogmatic citation, I jumped in with, "There is only one true faith founded by God, the Catholic faith. Men started all others."

"Once a Catholic, *always* a Catholic," was Scrounger's rejoinder.

Not to be out-cited, he continued with the corollary, "There is no greater insult to God than when He grants you the gift of faith and you reject it."

I could almost sense my brain's memory neurons logging every detail of this night: The unambiguous contrast between the fetid tropical smells, the sweat-salted tastes, the bone-deep weariness, and the bonding exchange *inside* our eight-by-eight, sandbag womb; versus the view of the *outside* through the restricted opening of our low-ceilinged bunker. Outside was a void where stars salted the night's otherwise lightless shroud that veiled wartime threats, threats that, in turn, thwarted appreciation of the country's natural beauty. I wondered if the Apollo astronauts who, possibly on that very same night, were preparing for their trip to the moon by orbiting the earth. Did they have similar views of outer space through their tiny misshaped windows?

"Damn. Good one, Scrounger-man!" I said. "My dad loved that one." I wondered how much to say about my father's repeated insistence ever since I had left the seminary that my eternal salvation depended on my return to Catholicism. He preached that it was as impossible to change my faith as it was to change the color of my privileged white skin. The Baltimore Catechism was intricately designed to lock in lifelong membership. "Ya don't want to piss off God," I added.

"Hell no, J.M. 'Cuz we all know, the source of all evil is (long pause) the *Devil*." He turned away from the opening to shield his draw on the Swisher Sweats. It cast a ghoulish glow on his long face in the lightless bunker and painted his red hair with an amber wash that matched the color of the Obesitrol bottle as he passed it to me.

I took a sugary hit and returned my stare through the bunker's window opening. Starshine winked off the outer Concertina wire. I wondered if my faltering faith was treading on my friend's. But the stimulant ramped up the recitation of the axioms that shaped our worldview as children, a view that included spectacular supernatural beings and miracles, a fully explained ancient past life, and an absolutist afterlife.

"Hey, J.M., do you think we still have our guardian angel by our side?" asked Scrounger, his voice dusted with the manly soot from the cigar.

"Ha! Maybe *you* do, but I bet mine was too damn smart to volunteer for this shit-show."

I swatted the ten-thousandth mosquito and realized I had been restlessly clicking my M16's selector switch back and forth from SAFE to SEMI to AUTO. I slathered on another layer of bug juice and sensed the skin pores on my face, ears, neck, arms, and hands drown in the goo as they ceded their attempt to cool me down in the night's heat.

"Okay, what was the one where the Pope can't tell a lie?" Scrounger asked, juicing the dialogue alive.

"*Ex-cathedra*, my man! God will prevent His Holiness from telling a lie on matters of faith or morals." My high school seminary training gave me the dogmatic high ground. "Nothing like having a monopoly on truth."

We were twenty-year-olds, not even needing to shave yet, grappling with the moral imprintings of our childhood and the foundational rebars of TRUTH. We had witnessed the defoliation of the land, the bombardment of villages, the murder of civilians, the torture of two young men, and the literal shredding of two small boys. We had guessed the names of body parts dismembered by our mortar rounds. We had fought, sacrificed, and risked our lives for a cause that was, at best, questionable. We had mourned the loss of fellow Marines. With assault rifles on our laps and a grenade launcher ready to repel possible intruders who might even live in the nearby village, we struggled with half-closed eyelids to protect our fellow Marines and survive one more night in a year of sleep-deprived nights.

We did not let down our guard.

Scrounger resumed the recitation of the *New Baltimore Catechism*. "When a person dies with a mortal sin on their soul, God sends them to eternal damnation in Hell." The lighthearted mood deteriorated as the dictate hovered like an invisible wraith of unspeakable jeopardy in the bunker.

"Well, Scrounger, did you ever meditate?" I asked, seemingly changing the subject, but not really.

"What?"

"Meditate. You know, sit still for ten or fifteen minutes and just think deeply about something."

"That seminary musta' fucked you up some, J.M."

"No. I was terrible at it, but one subject worked beautifully. Hell, and eternity." For a moment, I conjured the utterly silent peacefulness of the Borromeo Seminary chapel during our daily meditations. Our priestly instructors steered us towards topics like the grisly passion of Christ or the infinite love of God. Instead, I discovered that focusing on Hell's eternal torments suspended time. The specifics of the painful torments coalesced into a generic *bad*. Then I'd try to imagine this *bad* never ending. No, it has to end. Never ending. No, it has to end. Never ending! Over and over. A never-ending *bad*. Then time was up. Time to sing a hymn and go to class.

That particular doctrine ultimately led to the collapse for me of the moral house of cards defined in the Catechism. No crime fit that punishment. No god I wanted to believe in could be that cruel. Only humans are cruel enough to imbed that notion in children; humans who want to maintain control over them for life.

Like a tongue that incessantly explores the gap of a recently extracted tooth, I only sensed a hole where my childhood faith had served.

Scrounger stayed with the theme. "When a person dies with a venial sin on their soul, God sends them to Purgatory until the sin is cleansed. After cleansing your sins in Purgatory, you go to Heaven." Before I could butt in to supply the next piece of that lesson, he finished it. "Purgatory is just like Hell only temporary." I was ready for a very different lesson, but he was on a roll. "Prayers and a good life earn you grace, and grace can reduce your time in Purgatory." After Vietnam, he went on to become both a lawyer and an officer in the New York Society of

Certified Public Accountants. The Catechism must have served as his first accounting lesson:

---

†Heaven

Purgatory – (prayers + good behavior = grace) + some Hell-level torture

---

"Time for the magic show," I sing-songed, finally getting back into the conversation. "No matter how horrifically terrible the sin, if you're truly sorry for it, go to confession, and say the prayers the priest gives you for a penance, God forgives you."

"Yeah, I remember," he said rather solemnly.

"*Ego te absolvo a peccatis tuis.*"

No response.

"The magic words: '*Ego te absolvo,*'" I repeated. "*I forgive you.*"

Scrounger needed a poke and a toke from the Obesitrol.

"Even Hitler could have been forgiven if he asked for absolution," I continued. The theology conveniently ignored the victims of the sinners and whether they deserved a role in this absolution ritual.

I moved from the power of the Sacrament of Confession to the power of intercessory prayer. "If you offer prayers and good works to the saints and Mary, they can plead your case to God who might shorten your time in Purgatory."

Again, no response from Scrounger. Maybe the pervasive exhaustion of the war and the boredom of guard duty were overpowering the stimulant. Then again, maybe my cynicism was starting to scrape against his cherished beliefs.

Trying to resuscitate my friend, I whisper-sang the lines from Jimi Hendrix's cover of Dylan's "All Along the Watchtower:"

> There must be some kind of way outta' here
> Said the joker to the thief.
> There's too much confusion
> I can't get no relief.

The guard-duty irony was not lost on Scrounger. I leaned in and rebooted our Catholic memory game. "Hey man! How 'bout them saints?"

Revived, Scrounger complied sluggishly with more from the Catechism. "Saints are people who the Church knows are already in Heaven." I waited for him to recall the rest of the Catechism lesson. He came through. "The Church knew they were in Heaven because, after they died, miracles happened because people prayed to them to intercede."

"Fuckin'-A ri-i-i-ght, Mr. Scrounger." Amazing how deep dogma sinks into a child. "Remember the process? The Church has to confirm that the person was responsible for at least three earthly miracles." By now, the Obesitrol was really kicking in for me and ramping up my scrappy side. When the crash came, I knew it was going to be a hard one. "So, the concept here is that prayer, if done right, can change the mind of God."

"Whoa there, Mister ex-seminarian," he continued. Questioning prayer itself might have been a step too far for him. "No one changes the mind of God," he argued definitely. "He's all-knowing. He knows the prayers are coming and, if the guy deserves sainthood, He makes the miracles happen so the Church knows to make the guy a saint." Scrounger was adept at using the Church's theological slight-of-hand to support an argument. "Plus, there's that priest that has the job of exposing the fakes, right? The unworthy."

"Right. The Devil's Advocate," I offered. "But flip the argument a little. If you need a miracle—say, to cure your mother who has a terminal disease, why pray to a good guy who died just because you think he's saintly? Why not just pray to the guy who works the miracles, God Himself?" I took a breath. "Hey, my Mom needs a miracle right now and it sure seems more efficient to cut out the middle-man."

With a more somber tenor, Scrounger admitted, "I still pray. I pray a lot here. I pray I can keep a tight asshole in the next firefight. I want to get through this shit. I want all of us to. I pray for my family too." I could sense a tinge of antagonism in his voice. "I don't care if you think it's BS, it feels right to me."

"Hey, man. I get it," I said in a conciliatory tone. "I see prayer and meditation as extremely effective—for the person doing the praying."

Encased within nature's best soundproofing—sand—the heavy moist blackness, lit only by the muted glint of starlight off the grenade launcher's barrel, filled a long pause in the conversation.

"Let's move on," he said acidly as he crushed out the stub of his undersized cigar on a sandbag ledge. I followed his lead. My cigar's stale saccharine stench and counterfeit masculinity was insufficient for the task of imbuing the strength of character and courage I needed to face the lurking threat I imagined, cloaked with invisibility on this moonless night.

"OK, Sunshine. You know, this is just my guilty pleasure.

Just pokin' fun here. There's a flip side too," I continued diplomatically. "Strip away all the crazy stuff they fed me as a kid, and you'll find the core messages from Jesus." I gathered my breath and whisper-sang "All you need is love ... da, da, da, da, da." Maybe there was a little chuckle from my bunker-mate. "My parents laid the groundwork and the seminary imbedded ethics in me as deep as the molars in my mouth. Like the highest calling is to be in service to a worthy cause—something far greater than just 'lookin' out for number one.'"

"Pass me the speed," Scrounger ordered. "It's getting a little deep here, Slick."

"Okay, okay. Guess the Obesitrol's talking for me a bit. So, let's take on the real goofy one," I offered. "Limbo."

"Yeah. Number ten. Number ten, J.M."

"God sends non-Catholics who die without a mortal sin on their souls to Limbo after Purgatory."

Scrounger rose to the bait with another Catechism lesson. "Limbo is the same as Heaven, except you cannot see God." Then added, "Seeing the face of God is the best part of Heaven."

My ass needed a break from the illumination-round boxes we used as seats, so I stood up to stretch. Even in the near total darkness, I could make out details on the interior of our sandbag sanctuary, two canteens and cloth bandoliers for my M16 and the 40 mm grenades, the grenade pit in the rear corner, and, a few inches above my head, the black corrugated steel sheets that held up two layers of sandbags on the roof. Flexing eyeball muscles by focusing on close views helped relieve the stress of constant views into the near-featureless abyss of the night's void.

It was clear how this stuff was infused into the moral DNA of our childhoods with the same structural importance as brushing our teeth, or finishing all the food on our plate, or the command, "Don't touch yourself there."

I brought up the Church's salvation insurance policies. "Mary promised that she would personally intercede at the hour of death of any Catholic who completed the Nine First Friday or the Five First Saturday rituals of prayers and attendance at Mass." With false bravado, I declared, "I'm covered. Did them all in the seminary. Several times over. There will be pie in the sky when *I* die!"

"I might be fucked," Scrounger lamented softly.

Einstein predicted that time slows as the velocity of an object approaches the speed of light. Without human interaction or some kind of spur, middle-of-the-night time on guard duty crawls at a glacial pace. The incessant need to focus ears and leaden eyes on the limitless blackness beyond the Concertina wire for starlight glints off AK-47 barrels or telltale sounds of enemy sappers saps the body's energy like the gravity of a black hole sucks the light off nearby stars.

Pinching skin worked for me. Had I remained Catholic, I could have offered the pain up to Jesus, earned some grace, and traded it in after death to shorten my time in Purgatory (presuming, of course, I wasn't already in Hell, which was a fair presumption given I had already served my time in hell on guard duty).

One more gulp of the stimulant for both of us, and our name-that-dogma game got us through that double four-hour watch. These stretches were the hardest since they were preceded by night after night of limited snatches of fitful sleep in that combat zone.

"Okay, I got one," I piped in, trying to revive our keep-awake discussion. "Since Adam and Eve first sinned, only three people have been born without the Original Sin we inherited from them: St. John the Baptist, the Blessed Virgin Mary, and Jesus."

"I forgot about John the Baptist."

I continued, "Also, the Church says that Mary and Jesus ascended 'body and soul' into Heaven. Right?" Scrounger agreed. "So," I continued, "if you got three people with bodies up there, and you got all those heavenly pleasures —including good bodily chow … right … ?"

"Not sure where you're going with this, J.M."

"Well, where there's good food, there's *boo-coo* shit. I'm guessin' some dude's Purgatory time is up in Heaven burnin' shit just like we have to here in this shithole."

"At least in Heaven, it's holy shit!"

"R-i-i-i-ght, Scrounger! Fuckin-A right."[7], [8]

The Inquisition

Not surprisingly, something else began to stir in me especially during the very end of my senior year in high school. The most powerful motivator for the metamorphosis of my beliefs was not a more objective history lesson, divine inspiration, or intellectual gymnastics. From my lofty seminary pinnacle, I could see my future; and at Mass one morning, I realized that while Jesus may have given me the gift of a vocation, he neglected to include the gift of celibacy. Since, for the Catholic priesthood, you cannot have one without the other, I knew I was done with the seminary. In spite of the Church's policy against contraception, it tried to put a condom over my budding sexuality, but my hormones lurked like a nuclear sub under the icecap. Waiting. Every girl I saw took me to the borderline of a cardinal sin just because of what I thought. It was sex that gave me the laboratory to test the experience of love against the theory of sin. I wanted sex and a family, and I was willing to readjust my moral compass to get it.

I graduated a week or so later with good grades, and my father, who was a very influential man, was somehow able to get me enrolled in the well-respected School of Architecture at Kent State University in Kent, Ohio. It took me a long time to catch up with my non-celibate classmates, but I did fall in love with another Catholic student at Kent. I called her *Bridget* in my prior book. The cliché, "falling in love," is a poor descriptor of the process. Slowly, over more than a year, Bridget and I became explorers, the first to discover first love. We felt no one else could possibly have experienced that same dizzying, narcotic state of all-enveloping passion. We shared all of our sexual firsts together as innocents. It was respectful, deliberate, and loving.

Just as sex (or the lack thereof) was the main reason I left the seminary, the loss of our virginity to one another accelerated the loss of my faith. I could not perform the Orwellian trick of doublethink and accept both the Catholic Church's notion that the same God that would create us in his image and make us capable of a love so pure and enrapturing would condemn that love and us to Hell and an eternity of unimaginable torture. The punishment did not fit the victimless crime.

Something had to give, so I removed the "Fornication" card, and the entire Catholic dogma house of cards became unstable. It was a foundational card that was tied in by doctrinal rebar to so many other sex-related cards: "Male-Only Priesthood," "Celibate Priesthood," "Male-Dominated Hierarchy," "Missionary Position Only," "Anti-Birth Control," "Anti-Homosexual," and "Virgin Birth."

I had begun a new course in my education, and the theme of the course was that everything I had been taught since a child contained the elements of a lie. Ironically, Catholicism gave me the primer for creating the universe I wanted to inhabit. The religious world of my youth had a rich two-thousand-year history replete with wonderfully creative stories that included miracles on command, an afterlife, supernatural beings, a vengeful god, anthropomorphized evil, a righteous and loving savior, a near divine mother figure, divinely inspired scriptures, unfathomable mysteries, and infallible leaders. Once jump-started by sex, my seminary training was the ideal preparation for my religious journey. My first task as I matured was to transform the superstitions of my faith rather than replace them. In time, I learned to appreciate the mythology and treasure my nostalgia.

My old friend and mentor, Duncan Baird, who died at the age of 95, told me something about the Church and rules that he learned as the captain of a sub-chaser during World War Two: "The Catholic Church is the most successful organization in history. But if you follow the rules, you get chaos, just like the Navy. If it weren't for 'midnight requisitions' of the supplies we needed, we would've never gotten out of port to fight the war."

Compared to Catholic dogma, it was a much less imaginative leap of faith for Bridget and me to convince ourselves that the love we felt had to be as natural and as holy as any our Church sanctioned for its married believers. Freed by this modern Reformation, we defied eternal damnation with arrogant impunity. This led to an event that changed my life.

Soon after Bridget and I lost (or gave) our virginity to one another, it seemed like God chastised us. It was the start of the Christmas holiday and we told her parents we would be at my parents' house, and told my parents that we would be at her parents' house. Instead, we spent our first night together at my house. Some might say that God sent Cleveland a blizzard to delay our expected arrival at my parents' house, then my parents called hers to check when we left. Our ruse was blown. Caught *in flagrante delicto.* My parents were furious. We found ourselves in the gun sights of my father's withering gaze. What followed was two days of interrogation that would have impressed the CIA's rendition program. We named it the *Inquisition.*

First my father, playing the role of Torquemada, grilled both of us on the details of our actions and lies, and he preached of our evil intent. To my embarrassment, he even told Bridget how my seminary buddies and I had gone to see a dirty movie at downtown Cleveland's infamous burlesque theater, the Roxy. It seemed like God punished me back then too for that sexual transgression by making my wallet slip out of my pants pocket and fall behind the decrepit theater seat so that a Roxy employee could find it, call my home, and squeal on me to my mother before I even discovered it missing. Ever since, I inflexibly check for my wallet when leaving a theater seat.

It was Mom's shift next, and I could read her disapproval like a page of newsprint. But she lacked Dad's religious zealotry, so she sent in the two Catholic priests, long-time friends of the family, who were staying at the house over the holiday. With their professional skills at laying on the guilt, the two days became a tag-team match of inquisitors. The overall effect was a coordinated frontal attack aimed at deprogramming us from the clutches of a cult, the diabolical anarchy of the '60s. They had the advantage, the high ground, because thanks to my parents and my church, I was well trained in the fine art of obedience; a preemptive strike that neutralized any chance of demurring. Besides, silence was my first instinct. I went into a fugue state, my natural place of refuge.

At the start of the *Inquisition*, Bridget and I were young adults enraptured in the hot but normally short-lived flame of infatuation. Two days later, we emerged as two people welded together by shared adversity and a common enemy, on a mission to free ourselves from the oppression we perceived as endemic to our parents' generation. There was righteousness in the struggle. This event precipitated a falling out with my parents from which I never recovered.

I cancelled my birthright membership in the Church that used its cross symbol to crucify all competing ideas, and I became a religious orphan. The most formative period of my life up to that time took place over the three years between the ages of seventeen and twenty-one when I morphed from seminarian, to architecture student, to Marine, to agnostic. There are no secret passages to understanding. No magic words. I was like a shellfish that had to leave its shell to grow and enter its most vulnerable time until it grew a new home. The *Inquisition* was a gift. The faith of my childhood served as training wheels for my freewheeling exploration of deeper meanings as I birthed my own inquiry down a religious path that began in a spiritual desert for the next decade, but eventually led to my present state.

1968—Personal And Societal Chaos

I envied the moral certitude of my parents' world that the "Good War" had shaped. Instead of their black-and-white views, I faced an ambiguous blur of contradictory concepts, confusing events, and difficult questions. Historians are still trying to create working explanations for the debacle we call Vietnam.

My college courses required far more than forty hours a week. Since my father refused to help me financially after the *Inquisition*, I struggled to find enough part-time work to pay living and school expenses. TV news broadcast the chaos of the times. Success in Vietnam seemed tenuous after the disastrous TET Offensive in January 1968, which is considered the turning point of the war. Two months later, President Johnson admitted the war was unwinnable, and he announced his decision not to run for re-election after nearly losing the New Hampshire primary to antiwar candidate Sen. Eugene McCarthy. Meanwhile, Defense Secretary McNamara and the generals escalated the pro-war propaganda campaign. Assassins took our heroes, Rev. Dr. Martin Luther King Jr. and Sen. Robert Kennedy. Police beat down antiwar protests at the Democratic National Convention in Chicago and at massive protests all over the world. The so-called "Peace Candidate," Richard Nixon, sabotaged the Paris Peace Talks (known as the "the Chennault Affair") to defeat Hubert Humphrey for the Presidency.[9] About half of the 57,000 US deaths occurred during his subsequent terms.

I simultaneously thought I understood what was going on in the world while realizing I really didn't. I was conflicted and confused. I was not able to see the war as the act of US aggression it was. I could not muster the conviction to oppose it, even though by that time trusted leaders like Dr. King had already spoken out against it in 1967 (stating that the U.S. government was "the greatest purveyor of violence in the world today"), and Gallup polls indicated that a majority of Americans thought the war was at least a mistake, if not immoral. Although the horrific My Lai Massacre had occurred in 1968, it was not made public until the following year.[10]

Five months after the *Inquisition* in June of 1968, my relationship with Bridget was on the rocks, the relationship with my parents was getting even worse. I went on academic probation because of my lousy calculus grades, and my Cleveland draft board was about to reclassify me as "Class I-A: Registrant available for military service." I sensed (accurately) that the war was not going to end any time soon (the U.S. withdrew in defeat five years later). Even if I could have pulled up my grades by giving up my dream of becoming an architect, a field I later learned did not suit me, I could not see working my butt off paying my way through school only to be drafted after graduation and die in Vietnam. Plus, I figured the GI Bill would make school easier.

"October 18th," my birthday, was in the fifth little plastic ball drawn for the Vietnam draft lottery in December 1969. Because I lacked the courage and an anti-war conviction, I didn't stand a chance of avoiding the draft, but I had the perfect draft exemption at that time. I was already slogging through the jungles of Vietnam on search and destroy missions.

Rite Of Passage

The final reason for my enlistment was psychological: Seeing the daily news of the war with kids my age coming home in boxes gnawed at my conscience. I felt somehow that they were there in my place. Part of this psychological component of my decision was an aspect that I only realized when I began to write *Fire in the Hole* twenty-five years after returning home. It is the single most compelling motive for my going to Vietnam. I wanted to go through the traditional male rite of passage, the *hero's journey*. Here is a passage from my book that describes this important point:

> After nearly three decades of silence about my experiences in Vietnam, I found the Hero's Journey model and it has helped me to understand and integrate my experiences. The model involves five stages beginning with (1) a hero who, out of a sense of duty and honor, (2) undertakes a mission or quest. The hero endures a difficult test during the journey and accomplishes a valued mission, or at least makes a heroic effort, or dies trying. The hero (3) grows from the experience and (4) returns home with something the community values, and this is, at least ideally, then answered by the community in (5) welcoming the hero back home. The model works for many of the myths that are foundational to our cultural heritage, including the adolescent rite of passage.
>
> The first stage involves the hero, someone who commits to something bigger than himself or herself. The hero is willing to transcend thinking of self-preservation and undergo what author, Joseph Campbell, calls "a transformation of consciousness ... a redemption."
>
> Stage two, the quest, is a series of adventures and tests that are beyond the ordinary. It's a cycle, a going

and a returning, the death of one life (for example childhood and adolescence) and the birth of the next (adulthood). Childbirth, for example, fits this pattern perfectly, with the mother giving over of her life for the life of another, the rigors of pregnancy, and the pain of the birth process. It is definitely a heroic deed. For men, going off to war is just as timeless an example.

Cultures throughout history require that young men experience the warrior's quest as a rite of passage, an initiation rite to manhood. The hero leaves the realm of the familiar and descends into a dark unknown. There the hero learns important things, basic things about life, and the incredible range of human behavior. The warrior puts on a uniform and becomes a different creature. This is stage three. When I was a young man, I wanted a test, a dangerous mission that would help me prove to my father, my girlfriend, and especially to myself that I was tough and brave, or at least not a coward.

Stage four brings in the larger community. It's at this point that the Hero's Journey model broke down for the Vietnam veteran. Society has the responsibility to judge the value of the quest. The poet, Archibald MacLeish, speaks to this in his famous poem, "The Young Dead Soldiers." He has the young dead soldiers say to society, "We leave you our deaths. Give them their meaning." Well, America gave us the meaning of Vietnam. She decided it was at best a horrible and unfortunate mistake, and probably immoral. That condemnation poisoned the quest and the warriors. For decades, I was plagued by the question, could soldiering be moral in an immoral war? Now I realize the moral ambiguity that is inherent to all wars makes that question irrelevant to the combatant. [11]

The *Inquisition* was the first step on my hero's journey. I left my family and community to take on a challenge that involved risk by abandoning the strict sexual morays I was raised with. There was the risk of pregnancy and the inevitable deep loss that crushed my spirit when the infatuation died. Unfortunately, I lacked the maturity and wisdom to see the shallowness of society's equivalent strictures on traditional manhood, and the depravity of our Empire's war on Vietnam.

Going to Vietnam was an elephantine mistake.

Keep On Firing

Recently I watched *The Dirty Dozen,* a movie I hadn't seen since it first came out in 1967. It starred Lee Marvin as an Army major charged with executing a mission behind enemy lines. Since it was probably a suicide mission, he was ordered to train twelve incorrigible soldiers who had been sentenced to death or long prison terms for their crimes. They were expendable. The movie stars playing the criminals, like Charles Bronson, Jim Brown, Telly Savalas, John Cassavetes, and Donald Sutherland, had iconic roles that sprang from our country's social problems —bigotry and racial inequality, poverty, lack of education, religious fanaticism, and deranged cruelty. Most of the movie focused on how Lee Marvin, in perhaps his best-known role as the tough but fair father figure, tapped each man's hidden talents and motivations and molded them into a crack fighting unit. They completed the mission but only three survived, including Marvin. The rest of the men died and, with the exception of the religious fanatic, they died heroically.

Watching this movie again helped me remember my youthful patriotism and the optimism that heroic figures like Lee Marvin's character could accomplish great things and overcome America's shortcomings especially in the crucible of war. In real life, Lee Marvin, like my father, served in the Marines in the Pacific Theater of World War Two, and Marvin was wounded twice in the Battle of Saipan. My county was at war at the time, so one year after seeing the movie, I joined the Marines and went to Vietnam. I was nineteen.

I soon learned Vietnam wasn't at all like Hollywood's portrayal of World War Two. Fighting in the jungles and the rice paddies against people who were trying to kick us invaders out of their country didn't square with the pro-war propaganda my government had fed me.

I felt betrayed; but I kept on firing.

4. THE WAR BEFORE THE WAR

If we were to observe the soul of the family by honoring its stories and by not running away from its shadow, then we might not feel so inescapably determined by family influences.

—Thomas Moore

When families fail, common themes emerge: Distant fathers, far too busy, overburdened, and full of rage. Mothers who think the family will be better off if they just keep the secrets and just wait for things to change. But secrets fester and become infected. Only the truth, however hard the truth may be to tell, will staunch the wound. Only truth allows the healing to begin.

—Reverend Rob Eller Isaacs

It is important, if you grew up in a dysfunctional family, to take time to reflect on the competitive edge it has given you. People from happy, harmonious homes may feel healthy and well adjusted, but they're fixed on one family model, which they try to emulate the rest of their lives. If you grew up in a dysfunctional family, however, you may be deeply damaged but you've acquired a broad repertoire of negative models to outgrow. As you go about your adult life, you should thank your parents: they have given you the kind of education that happy children, through no fault of their own, never receive.

My parents taught me everything I need to unlearn.

—Andrew Boyd, *Daily Afflictions*

I wait in the small, windowless sitting room outside Thomas's office. The lighting is low, subdued like the worn furniture. I am alone with a stunted palm tree in a too-small clay pot; a puny bonsai version of the majestic areca palms of Vietnam. PTSD had stunted my emotions for three decades, but with Thomas's help, I am cracking my too-small clay pot.

The memory of the last session and its aftermath are still raw. I sensed disapproval in the look on the face of the woman in the waiting room when I left Thomas's office. How did she know? For the third time after leaving his office and driving to work, I couldn't get out of the car.

At least in Vietnam, I had a mission; I was skilled and well-armed and the men in my platoon had my back. Last week I couldn't walk to my office and deliver the appropriate greetings with a tear-stained face and attempt a normal day. It didn't matter that none of my coworkers knew much about my life beyond the walls of City Hall where I worked as a City Planner. I still imagined that they somehow knew that when my fellow Marines tortured those two boys, I DID NOTHING.

I couldn't face them, so I restarted the car and drove home to Cynthia's non-judgmental arms.

After a few sessions with Thomas, he again asked me to describe my crashes and if I sensed being at a different age while in their clutch. I realized for the first time that the debilitating sadness and inadequacies that periodically engulfed me matched those when I was eight to ten years old, the same ages as the two Vietnamese boys we slaughtered from our guard towers. With the accuracy and persistence of air-to-ground missiles aimed at old hurts I had buried deep in psychic bunkers, Thomas launched a series of questions. Like a witness under cross-examination, I answered factually never revealing my twisting gut muscles.

The facts were sufficient for Thomas to come to a judgment. He said we first had to deal with childhood issues before returning to Vietnam. "You could take any one of your wartime experiences, and the person on your right might blow it off completely and the person on your left might commit suicide over it. It depends on the person." He said my psychic wounds from war were the cause of my PTSD, but that my healing also depended on addressing the earlier trauma—childhood harm—that had not healed properly. In the years since completing therapy, every vet I know who completed talk therapy for PTSD described also dealing with childhood issues. Thomas said it was as if Vietnam had re-fractured a knee that had not healed properly, so complete healing was impossible. In the safety of his therapist office, he said we would fracture it a third time and carefully nurse it back to health. "You will still walk with a limp—there's no complete cure for PTSD, but you'll walk fully upright."

Most of my hundred-plus pages of therapy notes dealt with my childhood issues, as did most of my therapy sessions. As I explored my childhood, trying to relate puzzling scraps at the margins of my memory, I felt like a soothsayer attempting to interpret the entrails of a goat. I was so walled off emotionally that if someone asked me to get in touch with my feelings, I'd ask for a map.

When I described my upbringing to Thomas, I felt pathetic, like a self-indulgent child complaining about a life that was charmed in comparison to so many others. Thomas told me, "You are articulate, bright, creative, and strong, and you have your story down pat. You've built a terrific personality and a life full of accomplishments and wonderful rewards. But this has worked to cage an older thing that has stewed all these years, imprisoned by the success of the rest of your life."

Then he described the analogy that became the focus for the next six months: "You have trap doors that drop you back into the sadness of your boyhood home where there is another Michael who is timid, weak, and very emotionally damaged; a vulnerable boy, locked in a closet." Ironically, the coping skills I developed as a child helped equip me to deal with Vietnam while I was there, but, after returning home, these superior coping skills were a hindrance to healing.

Thomas said, "You've had a lot of practice at being disconnected and rational, but we need to explore the part that is not rational. One of our jobs is to get Michael to cry for Michael as a small boy. This small boy must be embraced with patience and Zen-like meditation. He has not been free to tell his story. He is the truth teller."

Referring to my emotional crashes, he said that part of our job was to de-link the emotion of sadness—he called it the "voice of the tender-hearted boy"—from its companion "buck-up" notion, which he called the "voice of the harsh boy." He added that later we would integrate both voices.

Childhood History—The Standard Version

I struggle to write this part of the story because of the mix of strong positive and especially negative emotions.

Just as every vet I know, including myself, minimizes the scale and effects of their combat experiences, I do the same with childhood problems. As Cynthia writes in her book, *Shockwaves*, "To highlight one type or cause of trauma over another, risks creating a hierarchy of suffering that I seek to avoid in this book. To say one experience or story is not as bad as another is to diminish the person and the pain. As the spouse of a survivor of the Oklahoma City bombing put it, 'You just can't quantify grief.'"[12] What's important is whether and to what degree trauma has long-term effects.

My emotional maturation process is still ongoing. The book that proved to be essential at the time of my therapy was, *I Don't Want to Talk About It*, by Terrence Real. It helped me understand how my father's actions had long-lasting effects on me. Equally important, it helped me to comprehend what shaped my father and *his* motivations, and to develop compassion for him. John Bradshaw's book, *The Family*, also served as an extremely valuable source.

To supplement what I write here, I've included longer excerpts in the Appendix at the end of the book. I encourage readers to explore these helpful books and benefit from them as I did.

My *public* story about my life was always positive. For Vietnam, it was essentially, "I survived. So many others had it much worse. I'm fine," which parallels the standard story of every vet I ever met. The same is true about my upbringing. I told Thomas how rich my life has been since marrying Cynthia and Jessica in 1973. I told him about our wonderful family life; Jessica's success in life, our excellent health, the meaningful work that we love and the financial security it provides, our rich spiritual lives, and our vibrant community of loving friends and family. I explained that I could trace the roots of my fulfilling life to many things including my childhood.

I grew up in middleclass America devoid of financial concerns. My parents provided an excellent Catholic education, great health care, and a beautiful home in a safe neighborhood that was chock full of kids able to have outdoor fun without interfering parents or coaches. My mother worked hard helping Dad in his business endeavors and keeping our meticulous home running smoothly. Yet she still mustered the energy to play with us, and was known as the "fun mom," which made her a magnet to our friends. Both of my parents encouraged me in school, sports, friends, and especially music. Music, in fact, was at the center of the happiness we had in the family from my perspective. Our family music nights and Christmas carol singing are among my happiest childhood memories. Starting with piano lessons and encouragements to sing in choirs, my parents, and especially my father, instilled in me a love of playing and singing music; a gift that I still treasure.

All my life, I heard echoes of my father's valuable adages in my head: "Finish what you're doing before you start something else. Anything worth doing is worth doing right. If you want something done right, do it yourself." To provide for their seven children, my parents worked long hours every day. They had fun too. My father built a bar in the basement, and he and Mom would party into the night on weekends with family and friends. To judge only by the externals, I grew up in the perfect suburban home in the '50s.

Thomas did not say a word, so I continued talking about my parents, then dead for several years, and explained that they gave me all of the things I needed as a child, and I know they raised me as they thought best. Their methods, including physical punishments that would be seen as abusive by today's standards, were probably not unusual or extreme considering the times and their own upbringings. I pictured them both and mimicked them telling Thomas, "We did the best we could.

We worked our tails off to provide a nice house, clothes, food, schools, a good neighborhood, music lessons, braces, and sports. We had fun together too. Our kids lacked nothing. We raised them with a solid Catholic moral foundation." I knew they both worked incredibly hard to make this happen and I was thankful, but there were crucial aspects that were missing. Somehow, their methods damaged all of us kids. To some degree, this same damage extended to Cynthia and Jessica as it trickled down primarily through me.

"I'm sure that's all true," said Thomas. "This positive story has served you well all of these years, but what else is there? What was missing?" Put on the spot, I grew tense, as I tentatively began to tell the "story behind the story." "Well, for one thing, they were both alcoholics," I added, immediately feeling like I was breaching the unsaid family law of secrecy.

Sibling Memories

I've included material about my family life in the hope that my experiences and what I've learned about them may be of value to others. I learned that, like my PTSD experiences, the childhood difficulties I experienced were probably common and possibly even endemic to my generation and earlier generations. Nonetheless, I venture down this path with trepidation. I ask the reader to understand that there are many positive as well as negative aspects to my childhood, but that my therapy necessarily focused on the negative most of the time because I had long refused to face *both* sides, and it was becoming obvious that the negatives were still having an effect that was impeding my progress.

At Thomas's suggestion, I contacted my siblings to help me determine "what was missing" from my well-practiced, "everything was rosy" tale I had spun about my childhood. At the time of my intense therapy, I had one older sibling and four younger. We lost one of our brothers in a tragic car accident when he was just twenty-one.

Their stories filled some gaps in mine and confirmed most of my memories. I discovered that I wasn't the only one who remembered growing up in a house that was full of fear of our parents. I wasn't the only one who was too afraid to confront them. One of my siblings described Mom as a "marginally functional robot" and "under the influence most of the time" during the period when I was in grade school. I remember arriving home from school and, quite often, finding her either incapacitated or taking a nap to sleep off the effects of alcohol or valium —the tranquilizer that was so popular among housewives in the 1950s, it came to be known as "mother's little helper."

Another sibling described the "toxic '70s" when Mom "poisoned herself with alcohol," and Dad laid the problems on us kids by frequently asking, "What are we going to do about your mother?" Part of Dad's answer was to have more frequent binges of his own.

Another sibling described it this way, "When Dad snapped, in three days, he'd drink every drop of alcohol in the house—which was a lot—and pass out. We'd call his AA sponsor and he'd spend a week in the hospital. Then he'd cry and explain Alcoholics Anonymous to us and ask for forgiveness." I also remembered it that way. Vividly.

My older sibling described the household of our later childhood as full of insecurity and fear of Mom and Dad as authority figures, saying it lacked love. "I was afraid to bring a friend to the house because of their drinking. There was no longer friendship or playfulness, only the rules. Neither of them ever helped us with homework, read to us, tucked us in at night, played with us, or showed any interest in school activities." After a long pause, the story continued. "There was no tenderness or support for any of the feelings and wants of us kids. 'Just stay out of my way,' was Mom's typical rebuff if I ever tried to learn things from her like sewing and cooking. But these were the typical places that Mom hid her drinks." I got the same answer from Dad as a kid, "If you want to help; stay out of my way. You can clean up afterwards."

My sibling continued with memories about dinnertime. "You remember, Michael. Mom rarely ate with us. Don't you remember how she typically took forever to prepare an elaborate supper, then burned parts of it, and then spent the entire dinnertime serving it? When we were all done, she would sit down to eat a few of the leftovers." (I remembered envying Mom because she avoided Dad's daily lecture about the evils of Communism, Democrats, non-Catholics, Jews, N-----s, etc.) "Remember how we kids all took turns doing the dishes because by that time, she had drunk all she was going to for a while."

My phone call had opened a floodgate. A long talk with one sibling had us agreeing that in the later years, we kids all retreated into shells and developed facades to hide our low self-worth. We had no sense of love and security, only fear and shame. We both remembered how Mom and Dad constantly bickered with each other, but felt empathy for Dad. He was no match for Mom who had the equivalent of a black belt in back-biting and, when on defense, her jujitsu-like taunts could emasculate Dad and his sputtering defenses. Only she could temper Dad's religious zealotry. We agreed on that call that for many years we thought a divorce would probably have been better for both of them because, together, they seemed to bring out the worst in each other.

"We became a family based on appearances." As my sibling talked, I could hear cracked words surfacing through tears. "I loved you so much, Michael, and then you went off to that seminary and abandoned me." It knocked me over that "abandonment" was just what another sibling had accused me of a few days earlier. In contrast, I viewed my high school seminary experience as an escape from the gravity of my parents' disease. I had to break out of my parents' orbit by clinging to the notion of a vocation.

One of my siblings had a different take on matters. "Turn to humor, it is the best medicine. Start writing jokes instead of horror stories and everyone, including you, will enjoy life better. Tell your therapist you and he are going to write a script and appear as a team at your local comedy club on amateur night. Take your veteran experiences, forget the savageness and the horrific, and remember the happy times and turn it into funny stuff." It was a half-serious suggestion from the sibling who played the comedian role in the family. Death came from alcohol thirteen years later.

One of my siblings sent me an email that commented on our childhood difficulties and on how we've been unable to maintain close relationships with one another:

I never thought I would have a problem with anything if I could survive that mess. As it turns out the biggest problems were Mom and Dad's alcoholism. I never envisioned having such a dysfunctional family at this point in my life because we were all pretty close as children. I guess we had a common enemy, Authority. Now we're on our own and there is no real bond, no family unity or even pride … . I'm in charge and responsible for my life and family and they are the most important things to me.

Our parents, especially our father, often pitted us children against each other. For example, in 1998, Cynthia and I celebrated our 25th wedding anniversary with a "re-wedding" ceremony at our church. When one of my brothers wanted to surprise us by showing up with his family, my father told him not to go because ours was not a "true marriage in the eyes of God" and should not be celebrated. Not only was ours not a Catholic marriage, he argued, but, since Cynthia had been married before, she was an "adulteress," as my father had referred to her behind our backs since our marriage.

An irony is that Cynthia's ex-husband had obtained an annulment from the Catholic Church so that he could remarry a Catholic woman, which thereby made Cynthia's marriage to me her "first" marriage in the "eyes of the Church." Seven months after coming home from Vietnam, I had married Bridget; a fatally flawed marriage that lasted only nine months. But it was a Catholic service and I had obtained no annulment. If anyone was committing adultery (or bigamy), it was me since, in the "eyes of the Church," my first marriage was still valid. Theological consistency (if not an oxymoron) was not my dad's strong suit.

Fortunately for us, my brother ignored my father's edict and his family surprise appearance made our ceremony all the more special.

To deal with our troubled home, our parents raised us kids with rules they added to the ones the Catholic Church devised: Don't ask, don't talk, don't trust, don't cry, don't get angry, don't be sad, stuff it, buck up, move on and get back to work, others have it worse, offer it up to Jesus (who suffered so much more), don't tell (family secrets), and—oh, by the way—strive for perfection.

Worse Than A Beating

I include the following story to illustrate the childhood atmosphere in the early Orange household. After I wrote it up, I read it to Thomas during one of our sessions. The spark for the memory came as I browsed through boxes of old family pictures after Thomas steered me to examine family of origin issues with a focus on when I was eight or nine. I went through the photos looking for buried truths and other landmines. It was the picture of Mary, the girl who lived two houses down from us that triggered the memory of this particular story. Her cute face brought back the memory of the crush I had for her. I think she felt much the same for me at the time.

The story involves my next-door neighbor, Eric. I idolized him and saw in him the characteristics I lacked and envied. He was older by four or five years, tall, handsome with wavy blonde hair, and heavily muscled. He exuded a self-assured confidence that the world was his to explore on his own terms. I soaked up a little of his Nordic god masculinity whenever he deigned to show me any attention. Eric represented the man I wanted to be some day (even though Eric was still a teenager).

The day of my story, Eric had a couple of his high school buddies over and they were hanging out in his driveway next to the tall hedge that separated his house from Mary's. Mary and I were playing together and joined them for some reason. I can't remember the particulars, but somehow, I felt one of Eric's friends had insulted Mary, and then Eric and the third boy joined in with snide laughter. Young student of chivalry that I was, I spoke up in her defense. Things escalated to the point that I became very mad and raced at the guy who started everything with my little fists flying. Like Eric, my target was a Goliath compared to me, but this was a fight he could not win. Squashing a little kid would have been only a Pyrrhic victory. Un-phased by my assault, he grabbed me by the front of my shirt, lifted me up, and hurled me into the top of the tall hedge. As I fell through it, scratched by the stiff branches and wet from the recent rain, my anger turned to rage—blind rage. In fact, the best kind of blind rage: justified blind rage. I raced at my assailant again and he repeated another artful kid-toss into the hedge. This happened four or more times until I heard all three boys laughing. Even Mary had lost interest by this time and left for home.

Spent, I headed home as well. I had stood up to the bullies and fought the good fight in defense of my lady. I felt the same elation as I did after seeing a heroic movie like Robin Hood. But the pain of defeat tainted the pride of my own heroics, even though the fight was not even close to being fair according to my standard, the Marquees of Queensberry Rules.

I went to the front door, which was odd. We kids learned at an early age that the front door was for adults and guests, not for kids, as was the impeccably clean living room the door opened onto. Maybe I felt this event changed me. On the other hand, maybe I just wanted to attract attention. I did attract attention because Mom met me at the front door and immediately saw my soaked clothes and that my shirt was ripped and bloodied in several places. She went off on her own blind rage about how hard she worked to keep us kids clothed and clean, how much money it cost to buy those clothes, and how my younger brothers needed to wear them after I outgrew them. It was after she calmed down a little bit that she asked what I did to get all those scratches on my face and arms. I began my explanation but she stopped me abruptly saying, "Your father will want to hear this." Normally Mom dealt with lesser offenses by lashing out immediately in anger. For the more serious crimes, she passed on the executioner's role to Dad, a role that, even as a child, I knew Dad hated.

It must have been a Sunday because my father was home from work. He added his scorn concerning the condition of my clothes and sternly waited for my explanation, probably thinking the whole time about the appropriate severity of the upcoming punishment. I clearly remember telling an accurate, concise, and unemotional description of the events. I was the noble victim who had acted heroically. I didn't need an impassioned defense; the facts would speak for themselves and the authorities would right the wrongs just like in the movies. However, my father didn't operate like the Hollywood sheriff. Instead, like Mom, he became furious at me. He would not even consider my point of view, and since I was too embarrassed to mention my feelings for Mary, he was blind to my chivalrous motive. He saw only the stupidity of attacking someone so much stronger. Like Mom, he was livid over my first-degree violation of damaging clothing, clothing he had worked long and hard to pay for.

He came to a quick decision about the appropriate punishment. This time, he didn't whip off his belt or even have to order me to go cut an appropriately sized switch from the "switch bushes" in the back yard.[13] No, the punishment was far worse. "You're going to apologize to those boys," he ordered. He took me by the arm before I could say a word (as if any of us kids would ever dare to say a word in confrontation), and marched me over to Eric's house where the three boys were still hanging out. I said something to Eric and his two friends that must have been sufficiently humiliating because my father was satisfied and we returned home. My mother demanded I change right away so she could wash and repairs my clothes.

When I finished reading the story to Thomas, he seemed to levitate straight up from his full lotus position on his chair and let out the biggest "wow" I ever heard come from him. He asked me how I felt when told to apologize. At the time, I thought it was about damaging expensive clothing, but I remembered how my parents looked at me with the glare that said you've embarrassed us, a mortal sin in their social religion. As a boy, I thought they should have seen my actions as I did, or at least simply advise me to avoid unwinnable fights. I told Thomas that my father took an event that I felt good about, because I had the courage to confront the boys, and transformed it into one that I then felt utterly defeated and embarrassed. When I disobeyed in childhood, the welts from his belt disappeared in a few days, but this unjustifiable condemnation stung well into my adulthood.

Thomas asked me to think about how I came to know as a boy that it was useless to defend myself passionately to my parents because they blamed me regardless of the circumstances. "This had the effect of depriving you of your potency. You learned that anger and defending yourself did not yield positive results. It was futile." He asked me to imagine what would have happened if I had stood up to my parents like I stood up to the boys by both presenting my case passionately and by refusing to apologize to the boys. I could not answer him. He brought the story's impact into the present time and said that PTSD relies on powerlessness. "Since you learned that nothing good can come from certain feelings—like anger, being in a bad mood, telling the truth about bad news, fear—you learned to win through externals."

Religious Wars

After I left the seminary high school at age seventeen, my primary childhood issues were with my father, not my mother. He lived for thirty-four years after I graduated and for most of that time, we battled over social issues like religion, politics, and lifestyle. When I think of him, I can almost hear a timer go off; the imaginary "bing" that rang after the first ten minutes of any longer conversation. It signaled the start of a subtle vibration in him, like the cry of overstressed steel, as he concentrated all his power on the age-old need to proselytize. To marshal his energy, he shut down the humane senses of compassion, understanding, and open-mindedness. Dad preferred to bark orders and demand answers in lieu of listening.

Dad had a game face for proselytizing as if the future of the Holy Roman Catholic Church hinged on my renunciation of my heathen ways and re-embracing the dogma of my youth. Dad was the consummate salesman, and the measure of his success was his ability to convince, to make the sale. The measure of the righteousness of his own religious and political beliefs was his ability to convince others of the same. The measure of the success of a preacher is the number of followers. He had none because his was always a demeaning sermon fueled by fear and hate. I can see Dad focusing his gaze and mind on infinity as he composed a new angle on the same old pitch. It was the gleam of something deeper than thought. It was the luminescence that accompanies absolute belief in dogma, the faith that makes saints and demons alike, that inspires the martyr and the murdering bigot.

The Catholic Church has a wide range of basic principles. Liberation Theology's focus on economic justice represents the most progressive manifestations of some of the core principles. In contrast, the Church's ideological obsession with sex led to positions that condemn birth control, divorce, and homosexuality; limits the priesthood to (theoretically) celibate heterosexual males; and condones the subjugation of women.

Dad's beliefs went way to the right of these conservative principles into unorthodox territory. He was pickled in the Catholicism of the latest Pope Pius. When confronted by the modest Church reforms of Vatican II in 1963, he regressed his dogma back to a time before science and democracy began to displace the Church's claim of authority over all in Heaven and on Earth. Eventually, his religious quest led him to a place that wouldn't fit even the Church's most conservative doxology. Dad was very successful at selecting guiding policies from both the conservative and the ultra-right wing of the Church. Like a compass finding north, he could point to written sources to buttress his all-encompassing belief in Mary worship; casual miracles; righteous social, racial, religious, and gender bigotry; and the "End Times" cult. He unquestionably relied on the Church's fundamental principle that it is the only true church for his belief that all non-Catholics are lost, probably evil, and most certainly deserving of their afterlife fate in the Church's fiery version of Hell. He might have supported separate public water fountains labeled "Christians (saved)" and "Non-Christians (justly damned)."

The "End Times" belief is that God is so angry at non-Catholics that he is going to destroy the world within a few generations. According to the movement's literature, liberal American Catholics may be the worst people on earth because they will conjure up and harbor the Antichrist who will then bring on the "End Times." When you consider that concept, it's little wonder that hatred for the people who were causing this enraged him. Dad lived in a world of only one truly Catholic person—himself, with righteousness his drug of choice. Just as he blinded himself during his pilgrimage to Medjugorje in the hope of seeing the promised "Miracle of the Sun" by staring directly at it, Dad was a victim of his beliefs and his desire to stay faithful to them.

Of course, religious stories are not about verifiable historical facts; they're sacred myths that provide orientation, identity, and community boundaries for a religious group. The Old Testament is based on an oral tradition of the imaginings of Bronze Age peasants. The uneducated, pre-scientific authors of the New Testament had their words censored, translated innumerable times, and edited repeatedly with political and economic pressures by the early followers of Jesus, then by Roman Emperor Constantine in the Fourth Century, and later by popes and kings.

Catholicism offered a smorgasbord of fertile stories for Dad that he either ignored or embraced as divinely inspired truth. Dad was a religious fanatic, but, underlying his fanaticism was an even deeper doubt, a dread of the eternal damnation his Church threatened him with; a dread that stayed with him right up to the unsettled time of his death. No amount of understanding, no amount of respect, no amount of evidence could have changed his mind or assuaged his fears.

After countless confrontations, I sent Dad this letter in the fall of 1995. He did not respond nor change in any perceptible way towards me:

Dear Dad,

I wanted to write you about some of the things that have been on my mind a lot lately. I'm writing instead of calling because I can express myself more clearly and you should have a better chance of understanding and recalling what I have to say. Our conversations have been difficult because you constantly want to proselytize. For these reasons, I don't expect to call as often but would rather establish a habit of correspondence instead.

I have always understood how important your religion is to you. I have always felt your faith is a wonderful thing for you. I learned as a teenager in the seminary that faith is a precious gift from God. I well remember during that period the tremendous glow of life that I felt because I was fully integrated in belief and in the practice of a religion. I know what faith is about and I continue to be happy for you and yours.

Because I don't have this same gift of faith, Dad, I don't share most of your religious beliefs. I have been open and honest with you when you ask questions about my spiritual beliefs. But I want to draw the line here and respectfully agree to disagree. I don't have a problem with you or anyone disagreeing with me. I accept and respect your beliefs as being good for you. I accept disagreement as healthy and natural. I realize that most people would disagree with my beliefs, and with yours.

You must understand that my spiritual quest is just as valid and just as precious for me as yours is for you. You and I both have a right to our own beliefs. Remember, we all have free wills. You do not have the right to impose your beliefs on me nor to be disrespectful to me. That is crossing the line. Problem is, you do this so many times. Since I left the seminary twenty-nine years ago, you have insulted and condemned my beliefs, values, life choices, and me.

Occasionally you also have done the same to my wife and daughter. I have had it. It has got to stop. If you cross that line again, I will let you know that you have done so and I will halt the conversation. I've tried ignoring it when you cross this line, realizing that your protestations only make me more solid in my beliefs. I've told you several times that your method is counterproductive. Instead of making your religion seem reasonable, attractive, and fulfilling, your proselytizing pushes others and me away. I've tried arguing with you. I've experienced anger and frustration and for decades I've realized the futility of it all. Nonetheless, I'm trying again with this letter to communicate with you.

Walk for a moment in my shoes. How would you feel if I said this to you: "Even though my religion teaches that faith in this religion is a gift from God and not everyone has been given this gift, nonbelievers are damned for eternity to Hell. Because you don't believe as I do and instead believe in something else, you deserve to be in Hell."

How does that feel?

You often ask what I believe in, and I tell you. Later you ask again and are amazed again at my answer even though it is the same as before. You don't care to remember. Well, I'll give you my answer this time in writing:

I believe that there is some Spiritual Truth, full and complete, and that the most profound mission of humanity is to discover more and more of this Truth and integrate it into living. Ten billion people have been on this quest for a million years and they have created countless religions as guides. I believe that most of these people have discovered some of this Truth, that no person or religion has it all, and that all persons and religions have some of it wrong. After all, they're just human beings and their religions are just human inventions. I have no belief in the supernatural. Instead, I believe the sacred is embedded in the ordinary. Philosophically I'm a Buddhist, socially a Unitarian, and religiously an Agnostic.

Some religions, including Catholics, some Protestant denominations, and Muslims, believe that they have the Spiritual Truth, the whole Truth, and that no other religion does. These religions believe that nonbelievers are condemned to Hell. Historically, in the most extreme cases, this belief formed the most fundamental rationale for one tribe to attack another. It continues today. Recently I saw a survey of the world's major conflicts.

Something like twenty-four out of twenty-seven had a religious basis: Moslem vs. Christian, Protestant vs. Catholic, Jews vs. Moslems, or one Moslem sect vs. another. Religious zealots use this belief in exclusivity to sanctify violence against the nonbeliever because they can portray them as an inferior people or even less than human. They use this same rationale to enslave people. This is a form of religious bigotry.

Things don't have to be as extreme as physical violence. You have used this form of religious bigotry for decades to isolate yourself and to reject people including your own family and friends. Now you seem to be trying to divide your surviving offspring into believer and non-believer groups and foster discontent among us. In the long run, you're bound to be just as unsuccessful as you are at conversions. Give it up, Dad.

You insult me when you think I insult you by not agreeing with your beliefs and by not being Catholic.

Sincerely,

Michael

Like the concept of the "inner child," I realize now that I have an inner father. The negative characteristics I saw in my father are part of my shadow self. They are the ones I have to work the hardest to overcome—intolerance, judgmentalism, stubbornness, selfishness, and moral superiority. I'd like to be different, better able to separate the mistakes people make from their worth as people. Terrence Real wrote about this in his book, *I Don't Want to Talk About It*. He said that sometimes a son would create the negative template of his father's life. He will hold his father in the very same contempt his father held his own father. "It leads to a vain attempt to be distinct from, that becomes the same as."[14]

Deathbed Conversions

I had a phone conversation with my father just before he began sinking precipitously towards his death two months later in 2000. I was in an Oakland hotel room with our daughter, Jessica. We had spent a fruitless and frustrating day in search of an apartment so she could attend graduate school there the following month. This is the essence of the phone conversation as I wrote it up a short time later:

"Son, this is your father."

"Hello, Dad. What's the matter?" Tired and confused, my mind raced over the fact that Dad had only called me once before and that was back in 1977 to tell me that my younger brother had been killed in a car accident. Nothing in my life ever warranted a call from him so I knew this had to be something in <u>his</u> life.

"I saw my doctor today—I can't remember his name—he's from India or some other God-forsaken country. Nobody speaks English anymore here. This country . . ."

"Dad," I interrupt him before he can launch into a tirade about the downfall of the US immigration policy. "What did you want to tell me?"

"My doctor ... he told me that my last stroke was the last warning. The next one will come at any time, and probably soon, and it will probably kill your father."

"Kill your father," I repeated silently to myself. A phrase so loaded with meaning yet all I could do was recall how Dad moved to the third person when he wanted to illicit sympathy. That third person language was always his style when he told me things like, "Well, Son, your father slipped a little," after he'd come home from a stint in the drunk tank at St. John's to recover from a three-day binge. Then I felt guilty for not jumping immediately to the sympathetic response he needed. After all, my father didn't have long to live.

"Are you there, Michael?"

"Sure, Dad."

"Well, I don't want to worry you. My sciatica's driving me crazy and I can barely walk to the bathroom to take a piss, but your father's OK."

Normally, Dad's voice sounded as if his vocal cords were metallic and his breath was a saw that scraped across them. You felt his words. But this time he was soft on the phone. Breathier and less rasping. I waited for him to continue.

"Are you there?"

"Yes, I'm listening. What did you want to tell me, Dad?"

"What?"

Louder, I repeated, "Go ahead, Dad." I hear the high-pitched whine of a hearing aid being tuned and a mumbled "damn things." With my war-damaged hearing, I'm an understudy for the hearing impaired.

"I want to take back everything I said. You know, when you and I fought just before Mother's funeral because I told you non-Catholics can't participate at her Mass. Well, I was wrong. I mean, who am I to judge? You said you've been searching for thirty years on these things —that's why I sent you all the material—to help you in your search. But it's not up to me. I shouldn't put any of my children in a category."

"Dad, you have me in tears here."

"Well, Son, I shouldn't be doing any of that stuff. I should be doing things that are nobler. You've got to find your own answers. I apologize for everything I said the night before the funeral. I shouldn't have said those things and I'm sorry."

"Thank you, Dad. This is very important to me. I'm sorry too for the things I said that hurt you."

"Good. Well, let's start over again, Son."

"OK, Dad. I love you."

"I love you too, Son. How could it be any other way? Bye."

I told Jessica what we said and couldn't hold back the tears. When I cry, I shrivel as my stomach tightens and my face squeezes in like an ugly imploded prune. Salty tears mix with warm snot. I don't like sobbing in front of my daughter but her firm hug gave me permission. "Wow!" she said. "He said that to you!? He said he was wrong all these years?! Wow! That's wonderful!" I called Cynthia back in St. Paul and she parroted many of Jessica's very words. The conversation *was* remarkable, wonderful, and incredible.

The next morning, I woke up and felt that it was bullshit. I felt Dad's apology was more to help him meet his "Judgment Day," than to help me. I wrote up the episode in my journal and concluded with this:

Deathbed conversions are crap. Nobody has the right to live one way, shit all over the people in your life, then, at the last moment, say, "Oh, by the way, I'm sorry for everything," and expect forgiveness and eternal happiness in the Paradise they believe in for themselves, just because they said the right magic words. Contrary to much of Western religious dogma, it is *this* life, not some afterlife that matters. Dad's apology and resolution to begin a life of loving-kindness were comforting but not sufficient. It won't wash. There, damn me and my family to Hell again, Dad. Go ahead. Go ahead. Dad ... ?

5. GOING DEEPER AGAIN

Many people prefer a comfortable lie to an uncomfortable truth.
—Patricia Roberts-Miller, *Demagoguery and Democracy*

True maturation on the spiritual path requires that we discover the depth of our wounds: our grief from the past, unfulfilled longing, the sorrow that we have stored up during the course of our lives … . Unhealed pain and rage, unhealed trauma from childhood abuse or abandonment, become powerful unconscious forces in our lives. Until we are able to bring awareness and understanding to our old wounds, we will find ourselves repeating their patterns of unfulfilled desire, anger, and confusion over and over again.
—Jack Kornfield, *A Path with Heart:*
A Guide Through the Perils and Promises of Spiritual Life

Veterans are the light at the tip of the candle, illuminating the way for the whole nation. If veterans can achieve awareness, transformation, understanding, and peace, they can share with the rest of society the realities of war. And they can teach us how to make peace with ourselves, and each other, so we never have to use violence to resolve conflicts again.
—Thich Nhat Hanh, *True Love:*
A Practice for Awakening the Heart

As I mentioned above, I struggled mightily with the childhood issues that were precursors to my combat-induced PTSD. My therapy sessions were necessary but not sufficient for enabling me to admit their full influences. I needed other teachers; experts on whose words I could rely. This chapter goes deeper with summaries of my most influential readings. I include it in the hope that it can serve as a helpful shortcut for others who have similar issues, perhaps as buried and camouflaged as mine were. The Appendix includes additional material.

The Father Hole

One day in the mid-80s, I happened upon the notice for a morning seminar for men as regards their relationships with their
fathers. At Cynthia's urging, I went. It was the first time I had
ever done anything like this. Dr. Ken Druck, co-author of *The
Secrets Men Keep: Breaking the Silence Barrier*, conducted the session. There were perhaps thirty men of ages ranging from the
early twenties to white-haired gents easily in their seventies. At
the time, I was pushing forty.

One thing I remember vividly was an exercise where we
paired up and took turns briefly described our relationships
with our fathers and then we role-played each other's father
using scripts we wrote for our partners. My partner was in his
twenties and, by my reckoning after we shared descriptions, had
a picture-perfect relationship with a father who should have
been played by Robert Young in the 1950s "Father Knows Best"
TV show instead of me. Following the script he gave me, I said
something like, "You've been a good son to me. I'm proud of you
and your accomplishments. I love you." Then I hugged him. To
my complete surprise, he burst into tears. When my partner followed my similar script and hugged me with the words, "I love
you, Son," I too crumpled into his arms shaking with long-sup-
pressed sobs. Like a snake that had just shed its skin, I wanted to
slink away from that reawakened vulnerability. Then I became
aware of the sound that surrounded me in the room; the sound
of grown men crying, all suffering like me from pandemic father
grief.

I knew then that the only way Dad and I could have a
meaningful connection was if one of us would die and be re-
incarnated as a different person.

Druck writes in his book about the same hole I felt for
as long as I can remember that I wanted my father to fill with
his love and approval. When he didn't, I began my campaign of

blaming him and seeking the approvals I needed from other substitute men.

At age thirteen, I sought out the company of men, holy men who taught at Borromeo Seminary. They welcomed me as a novitiate to their high priesthood. They tried to fill that gap in fathering. It was Father Bergliosi who raced me to the gridiron for our intramural football practices and then, repeatedly, had me go long for the pass. It was Father Schmidt who sent me sprawling on the basketball court. He didn't restrain his greater skill and size to pamper me. It was Father Brown who guided my hand for the silk-screened covers of the school's quarterly newspaper. It was Father Steward who trained my mind six days a week in the rigors of the Scientific Method. "There will never again be a conflict between the teachings of the Church and science," he preached. It was Father Wysinski who, more than the others, nurtured my love of learning, history, and reasoning. It was Father McLaughlin who trusted me with the leadership in my junior and senior years with the fifty-voice seminary choir. On the day I decided I no longer felt the vocation to become a priest, it was Father McLaughlin who accepted my decision and guided me on to the career path that has nurtured me ever since with passion and purpose.

Thank you, Fathers.

Childhood Trauma

Cynthia reminds me that grief and the other effects of trauma can be cumulative when you don't give each loss the attention it deserves. If not dealt with, grief can lie dormant until re-awakened and augmented by the next trauma. A stockpile of losses can lead to depression and other problems.

In their book, *Broken Toys, Broken Dreams*, psychologists Terry Kellogg and Marvel Harrison Kellogg state, "A trauma is an event or process which threatens life or life's meaning ... . A witness to trauma experiences the trauma." In confirmation of Cynthia's comment, they write that, "Unresolved loss hinders the forward movement of our lives." Their book describes the "betrayal of sanctuary" and its persistent effects. A critical conclusion in the book states, "Being hurt by those who should be protecting or nurturing us is a betrayal of sanctuary. This sanctuary betrayal is the most difficult type of wound to heal." Terrence Real points out that scientists are finding the neurological (physical) components of the concept of the "inner child."[15] Brain surgeons are able to stimulate specific parts of the brain and trigger the exact sensations and memories of a certain age level. Like the rings of a tree, each of our developmental stages remains intact.

After a lifetime of placing less trust in my feelings than in my thinking (or, more honestly, the thinking of the "experts"), statements like these provided the academic rationale I needed to finally admit what my heart knew all along about my childhood trauma but was too cowardly to face. Because this information is new to me and has been so helpful, I've included a fair amount of it in the Appendix hoping that readers who, like me, would not normally search out this kind of material, will find my synopses helpful.

John Bradshaw, the famous educator and author, writes in his outstanding book, *The Family: A New Way of Creating*

Solid Self Esteem, about the historical underpinnings of the typical American family. After describing the monarchial structure of most societies up to two centuries ago, he writes that family structure naturally took on this same monarchial structure. Although many societies matured over the last two hundred years with the spread of democracy and the notion of individual rights and freedoms, family structure did not evolve similarly until the social upheavals of the '50s and '60s began the process.

Bradshaw writes, "Our consciousness has expanded immensely beyond the sexism, racism, homophobia and emotional primitiveness of pre-World War Two patriarchy." This new shift in consciousness, he explains, exposes "the old patriarchal model of child rearing as abusive," especially the typical method for keeping children in line through "shaming punishment."

He cites a psychologist's description of "toxic shame" as "the most damaging form of domestic violence there is" and states that, "Perhaps for the first time we fully see that childhood abuse is the greatest social problem of our time." His depiction of the typical family environment prior to the 1960s matches perfectly the home I grew up in. "Parents were to be obeyed as if they were gods. They were to be honored. Children were never allowed to raise their voices or express anger towards their parents. Like the great monarchs, parents were held answerable to God .... Anger was especially forbidden and punished .... Anger is the feeling that gives us energy to fight those who violate us. Our anger protects our rights. The family hierarchy of power was blatantly nondemocratic."[16]

On the topic of blame, family systems theory as described in Bradshaw's book is similar to Alcoholics Anonymous thinking about alcoholism. Since alcoholism is a disease, the alcoholic cannot be blamed for having the disease, but they are fully responsible for taking the actions necessary for recovery and they are fully accountable for their behaviors. Similarly, parents and their children should not be blamed for the conditions within a dysfunctional family and the necessary roles the members assume because of these conditions, but, as adults, all are accountable for their behaviors and are responsible for seeking a healthy recovery. Surprisingly, Bradshaw writes that the process of becoming fully adult with a solid self-esteem can take forty years even without a dysfunctional family that creates a late start in the process and greater hurdles.

I agree with Bradshaw. I don't think Dad intentionally tried to hurt any of his children. Here's my 'armchair analysis' on Dad: His repertoire of behaviors were culturally limited. A key motivator for him was a deep fear of loss of control—control of his alcoholism (which spawned his workaholism), control of his wife and children (which was the source of his patriarchy), and control of his future (which led to his religious and political fundamentalism). When he wasn't on a drinking binge, his drugs of choice were workaholism and fundamentalism, which helped him deny the reality of his powerlessness over his disease, others, and the future. Unable to understand or tolerate the intensity of this emotion of fear, he chose denial and to see his problems as external. Then all he needed to do was to control the perceived source of his distress. He was not able to touch his own suffering so he acted it out on his children primarily through neglect and the toxic shame from the "poisonous pedagogy" Bradshaw writes about.

Dysfunctional Family Basics

In August of 2003, midway through my therapy for PTSD, I attended a weeklong retreat with Vietnamese Buddhist monk, Thich Nhat Hanh.[17] Also attending was an internationally renowned child psychologist with whom I discussed family of origin issues and PTSD (her husband is also a Vietnam vet). She said that effective parenting boils down to three essential practices: Nurturing, limit setting, and guidance.

My current gift of life, grandfathering our identical twin grandsons, allows me to observe what happens in a home that is rich in these three essential elements; a home where our daughter and son-in law meet the boys' needs with love and respect. In their early years, the boys squabbled over whatever toy the other one had and they had their difficult days. But their default setting, the setting they normally wake up to and stay tuned to was one of joy, and their joyfulness is infectious. When they were young, they woke up singing and spent most of their time playing happily with each other.

I love them with an intensity that brings tears to my eyes. They are delightful examples of children who blossom from just this kind of effective parenting—and grand parenting. The countless acts of nurturing, limit setting, and guidance fundamentally shaped their characters in positive ways.

I believe my parents created a nurturing home for me during the crucial first three years when, experts believe, the foundation for our self-image is grounded. Like our grandsons, my default setting is a positive, secure, and happy one shaped, no doubt, by the love of my parents and siblings. Change came later when the pressures of five more children and especially the ravages of alcoholism transformed my parents and our home life. It was then that they began to both starve me of nurturing and guidance, and flood me with limits.

Let's start with the first point—nurturing and its companion behavior, to love unconditionally. This is what I've since learned about unconditional love and the self-esteem it engenders: Healthy self-esteem is an inherent, non-fluctuating sense of oneself as being essentially worthwhile. The capacity to esteem the self arises from a history of unconditional love from one's caregivers. In contrast, my parents conditioned their love during this later period on good behavior and conforming thoughts.

The other essential aspect of nurturing and unconditional love is to send the message that no child is essentially better or worse than another. A healthy parent will not value one child more than another. Each will be the "gleam in the parent's eye." Instead, my parents played one child against the other, with especially damaging results for two of my brothers—the family "bad boys."

We are moved to action when we feel our shame. We are moved to joy when our needs are met. Because our emotions are forms of energy, we can only stop feeling them by mustering counter energy. We do this with muscle tension, shallow breathing, fantasies of punishment or abandonment and critical self-talk. This tensing, internal talking and shallow breathing are the ways we physically numb out. After years and years of practice, we can literally no longer feel our emotions. Psychic numbness is the soil out of which our addictions are born. Bradshaw concludes, "Our addictions are a way we can feel alive."

I so often wondered why, decades ago, someone more emotionally advanced than I didn't grab me by my shirt, slap me out of my stupor, and force me to confront these matters. Then I realized my wife had been doing everything but the slapping since she first met my family back in 1973. Also, the psychology I have been relying on only dates back to the late 1980s.

"A Very Serious Case"

So often throughout my therapy, I took my parents' side. I told Thomas my theory that to be successful, parents would have to accomplish a thousand things with their child. Since no parent can do it all, by definition then, every child will have some complaint how mom and dad are responsible for their problems. He replied with a story about a Robert Bly reading he attended. A father in the audience asked the respected Minnesota poet if he could do everything right as a parent, would the child turn out OK. Bly berated him with his characteristic pretentious belligerence and told the father not to burden his child with perfection. "You can't help but screw up your child in some way. It's inevitable. The best you can do is love them, do your best with the knowledge that it's inadequate to fully prepare them for the world, and do it with grace."

After I had explored my family history with Thomas, he stated that I suffered from a sufficiently serious case of neglect as to leave psychic scars. I staunchly resisted his assessment thinking that only physical or sexual abuse would have lasting effects. It took the work of the experts I've cited here who supported his conclusion to eventually convince me of the nature and power of the harm. I had to work to view my past from the child's perspective, not from my adult perspective.

According to the child psychologist whom I met during my retreat with Thich Nhat Hanh, studies show that of physical abuse, sexual abuse, emotional abuse, and neglect, neglect can have the most damaging, long-term effects on a child. She said that for many, childhood wounds never heal without therapy.

Thomas summed up my family description with an observation about the severity of the dysfunction in my family: "You know it's extreme when you have two alcoholic parents. You were damaged first at home to the degree that you fled it to attend a seminary and then you volunteered to go to Vietnam where you experienced trauma to a degree that you were unable to heal from." With a voice that seemed to come from somewhere deep down in a well, Thomas concluded, "It's a *very* serious case."

Pre-Psychological Generation

Recently, I heard a family therapist, Dr. William Dougherty, describe my parents' generation as "pre-psychological." He said my generation was the first "psychological" generation that had the benefit and the social acceptance for therapy. When we look back on our youth, we bring that psychological/therapy-based expectation with us, and yet our parents, especially our fathers, who grew up under the influence of the Depression and World War Two, wouldn't even have known what we were talking about or understand that such a need for therapy existed. Parents of that era usually had the "just buck up and move on" philosophy that caused them to suffer in silence.

It was true for Dad and me. Whenever he began his incessant religious proselytizing, we could have been talking in Morse Code across a cultural divide as wide as the Grand Canyon. Dougherty said that he and his fellow therapists can take any man from my generation and have him sobbing within forty-five minutes, "Crying because they feel entitled to a perfect father."

Claude Anshin Thomas, a Vietnam veteran and Buddhist monk, writes about how World War Two influenced my parents' generation in his book, *At Hell's Gate: A Soldier's Journey from War to Peace*: "Today I understand that my father and the men and women of his generation were filled with illusions and denial about how deeply they were affected by their military and war service. Having come home as victors, they were thrust into a role: They became the protectors of our country's denial about the profound and far-reaching impact of war—not just on those that fought, but on all of us. This cultural myth obligated my father's generation not to talk openly or directly about the reality of the individual war experience, and in a sense, for many of them, their inner lives had to be abandoned. Speaking truthfully wasn't encouraged in them or in me. But something unusual happened during and after the war in Vietnam: Many of us could no longer deny reality."[18]

Going through therapy with the expert help from my therapist, Thomas, the loving care from Cynthia and Jessica, time off work, and my therapy-friendly community, I acknowledged that my parents had none of these resources to help them break the chain of psychological abuse they inherited via the same patriarchal parenting rules they were inculcated with by their parents. The seed of such abuse was planted in their natures long before its acidic fruit spoiled our childhoods.

I think Bradshaw would agree. He writes that parents actually had no real choice in how they parented unless they first worked through and clarified their relationships with their own parents. Rather than communicate the unconditional love necessary for healthy child development, my parents' generation held to the old monarchial rule that if they clearly communicated to their kids that they loved and treasured them for who they were, they would "spoil" them.

6. TAKING THE LEAD IN OUR TROUBLED DANCE

Psychological trauma alone, neuroscientists now tell us, affects not only psyches but brains. Sophisticated neuro-imaging shows the brains of those who suffer from Posttraumatic Stress Disorder to be abnormal in areas regulating memory retrieval and inhibition (hippocampus), fearfulness and focus (pre-frontal cortex), and emotionality and [openness to change, adaptability] (amygdala).
—Gerald M. Rosen, *Posttraumatic Stress Disorder, Issues and Controversies*

Come on mothers throughout the land,
Pack your boys off to Vietnam.
Come on fathers and don't hesitate
To send your sons off before it's too late.
And you can be the first ones in your block
To have your boy come home in a box.

And it's one, two, three, what are we fighting for?
Don't ask me, I don't give a damn. Next stop is Vietnam.
And it's five, six, seven, open up the pearly gates.
Well there ain't no time to wonder why,
whoopee! we're all gonna die.

"I Feel Like I'm Fixin' To Die Rag,"
Country Joe and the Fish

E ventually, the visceral anger I harbored for so many years against my father abated. He died in 2000, and I have been more able to see how I sometimes had the lead in our troubled dance. Once we drew our battle lines, the slightest flaw or imperfect comment from Dad became one more rationale that built my case for my anger. My relationship to Dad was one of tolerance, not understanding; duty, not love; acceptance, not respect; rebellion, not loyalty. That was the best I could muster. I was not able to accept the father I had and instead searched for and found continual evidence to buttress my debilitating disappointment and anger.

For the last three decades of our lives together, my unacknowledged PTSD colored my relationship with my father, just as the generational influences I've described above colored his with me. I survived the war physically but came home with an even greater "father hole" because Vietnam had burned away my patriotic and religious beliefs and even my fundamental trust in the inherent goodness of people.

Dad could not get beyond our philosophical, religious, and political differences and see me as his son first and foremost—a son (and fellow veteran of war) who needed his love and unconditional acceptance, especially after Vietnam. That's one of the purposes of family—to expose you to people you wouldn't otherwise choose as your friends. Like the extreme need to urinate, if not fulfilled, peeing takes on an artificially intense importance. When satisfied, the importance evaporates. Those who had the father craving satiated as a child cannot fully appreciate the power of that emptiness for those who didn't get a healthy dose of the essential vitamin of unconditional love.

I wasn't any better. I refused to see my father, his motivations, limitations, and intentions any deeper than the bigotry and fundamentalism he spewed within ten minutes of any meeting. I needed a father to love but rejected the flawed one I had. I granted him great power over me through my anger at him for not giving me what I needed.

While I focused for so many years on the fact that Dad refused to accept me as I was and to love me unconditionally, I largely ignored the corollary, that a father needs the same from his son. I think there is a difference in scale of need, though. The son's need is born in childhood and can have the intrinsic intensity akin to imprinting; while the father's need for the son's acceptance and love competes with all of his other adult demands like career and other family responsibilities. While I had only one father to satisfy my needs, my father had seven children to supply his.

As I mentioned, Dad began his rejection of me after I left the seminary in 1966 when I was seventeen and began my serious quest for my own belief system, which quickly began to contradict his. We weren't the only actors in this intergenerational battle. The entire world was in upheaval at the time. Our two generations were engaged in social battles the intensity of which have not since been exceeded. Dad hated all of the "movements"—antiwar, peace, civil rights, feminist, prisoner rights, environmental, gay rights, free love. The list goes on. My generation was out to change the world his generation had saved from fascists and Communists.

His intensity of belief fueled my own. I had learned from him the importance of these matters. As an adult, I did try for so very long to agree to disagree in the realm of politics and religion in order to keep our conversations within safe bounds. However, once engaged, I rarely held back, so we'd typically fight our way to our respective ideological corners with only a rare compromise or concession. Everything we said to each other made us both dig in our heels more fiercely.

How might it have gone if I had told him more often what I respected about him and his life accomplishments? My father was very generous with his time, concern, and money for some members of our family and for the religious causes he supported. We also bonded on being the veterans in our immediate family, Dad in the Marines and Mom in the Navy, during World War Two.

It's easy to remember the hard times and harder to draw out the lighthearted ones—but here's one to consider.

Growing up, I loved hearing my parents retell the story of their first year of marriage. On the ship home from Guam at the end of World War Two, Dad came up with a money-making scheme. After their marriage a few months later, he and Mom traveled cities, big and small, throughout the Midwest. They'd check into a hotel and scour the Yellow Pages for the addresses of all of the social clubs (e.g., Veterans of Foreign Wars, American Legion, Moose, Kiwanis, etc.). Dad's pitch was to find the manager at each and ask if the war was hard on business. He'd weave in that the sign out front was outdated or in need of repair and that he could buy the club a brand new sign—one that was much bigger and better to attract the driving public, which was an exploding market. All he wanted in return was permission to set up a large board in a prominent place inside where he could sell advertising to the local merchants, many of whom would also become customers and possibly sponsors for club events.

Then he'd return to the hotel, design and order the sign, and he and Mom would hit the phones to sell the ads. When the sign was up, usually in a week or two, and they had sold enough to pay for the sign and make a profit, they'd drive to the next town. As the payouts improved, so did the cars, hotels, restaurants, clothes, and nightclub life. This lasted until the first baby was due and they moved to a burgeoning Cleveland suburb to started the family's first business, Orange Line Publishing, which earned them enough to keep our eventually large family in the upper-middle of the Middle Class.

Instead of expressing my respect for his fascinating history and selective kindness and charity, bitterness over his general disregard of *my* family silenced me.

I still ponder why Dad's beliefs were like a stone in my shoe. Why couldn't I simply let him be with his own ideas and simply move on? I knew it is so much more effective to speak for your own beliefs than to criticize someone else's. I mirrored Dad's deep desires and wanted a father who loved and respected my beliefs and me.

Recently, I described to a friend how a Vietnam veteran friend of mine seemed unable to get beyond the anger stage of dealing with his PTSD from the war. My listening friend, who is steeped in Buddhism, commented by asking rhetorically, "What keeps him stuck, and how is staying stuck feeding him? Does he value his victimhood?" Since we had previously been talking about the family work I had been doing, I internalized the questions and recast them as regards my angry relationship with my father. I realized how feeding my anger for more than thirty years freed me to stay disconnected from him. My anger made it easier to abandon my efforts to find common ground, interest him in my life, and foster an interest in his. When it came time to take care of him in his old age, especially during his last five years after Mom died, a younger brother and his wife shouldered that responsibility while I treasured my independence in my community seven hundred miles away. Yes, my anger and victimhood were very valuable to me, and I held on to them dearly. This writing is helping me let go.

Whatever wounds Dad suffered as a child, I don't believe he ever had the opportunity, education, inclination, or support to heal from them. Probably the biggest gulf between my parents' and my generation is that self-examination scared them to death, while I'm attuned to every quiver of ego and id. Part of Dad's legacy, unfortunately, was to pass on to his offspring the fear and pain that plagued him to his deathbed. Always true to his character, Dad was a force of nature; as unstoppable as the tides. Can we blame Mother Nature for the destruction she can cause?

My youngest brother offered some valuable insights. It's helpful to know that, after graduating college and marrying, he and his wife managed the family business, raised their two beautiful children in the Catholic Church, and stayed very close to my parents. They were our parents' primary caregivers all the way through their difficult lingering deaths.

Now, he is sixty, and suffers terribly from the same osteoarthritis that plagued our mother at a much earlier age. "I know the excruciating pain Mom dealt with for most of her life, and she didn't have the modern drugs that help me. Only her vodka." As for Dad, for many of his later years, he was on morphine-like pain medications including Percocet and others that can cause hallucinations.

My brother wrote the following in an email that summed up our parents' point of view:

> I've told you before, all the shit I watched growing up was incredible. Almost every one of my older siblings broke Mom and Dad's hearts with decisions they made. Mistakes that were so clear to them but not to their children's youthful optimistic eyes .... Dad and I grew closer after he got sick and he really was a good guy. He was constantly donating his money to causes he believed in and he was generous with his time and his love. I wish I knew him as a friend better rather than as a father. He had a good life.

I can understand his perspective. As a child, he saw Mom and Dad wisely predict the unfortunate results from the poor decisions some of their children made and my terrible decision to go to Vietnam. He saw them worry endlessly and helplessly about another sibling's alcoholism. From Mom and Dad's Catholic viewpoint, our religious choices were not only condemning several of us to hell, they must have seemed insulting to them as well. We flipped Dad's orthodox Catholicism on its head, one of us with fundamentalist Christianity and me with agnosticism. Another sibling delivered possibly the most painful blow by converting to Judaism, the faith of the people who, they believed, killed their lord and savior. Yes, we broke their hearts.

Rather than try to talk me out of my feelings of guilt, Thomas helped me recognize how responsibility and guilt were shared among all the parties involved.

Last Words For Dad

Over the last three years of my father's life, he battled congestive heart failure and survived five near-death experiences
brought on by his deteriorating health. Dad was so enmeshed
in his unique version of Catholicism that he was convinced that
any decision to forego a treatment that held some promise of
lengthening life was tantamount to suicide. Since Catholicism
claims suicide is a mortal sin deserving of eternal torment, Dad
believed his soul hung in the balance. His doctors kept offering
additional treatments and operations that extended the dying
process so, since Medicare paid for virtually everything, he
agreed to every option.

Finally, in 2000, he lapsed into a coma. As the family
gathered at the hospital, I asked if I could have an alone moment
with him. Sitting close to his face, I told him I was alone and then
said something like this:

Dad, I know you would probably like to have the chance
to give me some final message here if you could. It's OK.
Over my entire life, you have given me very consistent
messages and I have listened. You are the most influential person in my life. You have been like a hammer
that shaped me. Even if you don't exactly agree with the
shape I ended up as, it was still your influence. Since
I like the shape I'm in, I accept the process we've gone
through all these years.

I look at your situation and I can't imagine God would
want this to continue. I can't believe that refusing to
have more artificial tubes, drugs and IVs could be wrong.
I think God would say to you that it's time to relax. It's
time to let go, Dad. It's OK to let go now.

I love you, Dad.

Half an hour later Dad died.

Ever since I was a kid, I sought my father's simple approval. I never heard the words I wanted to hear from him—that he was proud of me, proud of the family I raised, and the life I've lived. How could he? He truly believed I deserved eternal damnation for rejecting my Catholic faith.

Years ago, Alka Seltzer had a commercial that went something like this: "We've invented a new disease, the Blahs. You know, upset stomach, headache, that all-over ache; miserable-to-the-core feeling. Fortunately for you, we've also invented the cure." Then came the product pitch. The Catholic Church of my youth was like this. The Church invented the disease, Original Sin. You know, the inherent worthlessness and sinfulness of every person at conception; miserable to the core of the soul. Fortunately for Catholics, the Church also invented the cure. Then came the product pitch. The pitchmen for Alka Seltzer only promised temporary relief if you bought their cure. The pitchmen for the Church promised eternal salvation if you bought their cure—baptism—and eternal damnation for those who didn't. Unfortunately, my dad had tremendous product loyalty to his Church. (For counterbalance regarding my relationship to my father, Chapter 12 includes several positive stories about my father.)

Mom

I've included so much of my writing about and to my father and have largely ignored my mother. Actually I've ignored both mothers. I feel like I had two of them. I've described the home-maker mom who somehow kept a perfect home for her husband and their seven children who loved her, while working long hours for the family business. That's the *June Cleaver Mom* that raised me until I was about eight. I remember feeling the deep pride whenever Dad would dress in his regal Knights of Columbus uniform, complete with top hat and a real sword, and Mom would complement her dress with two mink furs wrapped around her neck. They stepped straight out of a fairytale.

I also described how alcoholism helped birth a different mom in later years; a mom who was a Gold Medalist of Bickering with her husband. One sibling loved the fun-filled "sweet spot" period between when Mom was the strict but caring parent and when she was drunk.

The surprise was that, when away from her husband, my June Cleaver Mom was delightful, funny, charming, and very loving. My mother, Ruth, had a custom of not giving a name to be called by her grandchildren but instead inviting each to name her. Jessica's name for her, "Gruffie," fit well among the panoply of Gammy, Gummo, Grammy, and Grandma from her other grandchildren.

My June Cleaver Mom loved to play Three Strikes on our driveway basketball court, or show off her high school gymnastics skills. She played cards and board games with us kids and welcomed the neighborhood kids over for snacks. She could put a mean spin on the ping pong ball and do tricks on ice skates. In the time it took her to walk past a jigsaw puzzle, she'd put in a piece.

One of my younger brothers related a story when he and another brother were driving home one evening along Cleveland's Memorial Shoreway, probably in the early 1970s. Mom was in the back seat of her very cool (or hot), 1967 Ford Galaxie 500 convertible. When Mom lit up one of her Viceroy cigarettes, they offered her a hit on a joint instead. Mom hesitated but then stubbed out hers (ashtrays were right next to every seat in cars back then) and agreed to give it a try for the first time in her life. They switched the radio off Mom's AM news station to Cleveland's FM rock station, WMMS. The sounds of Led Zeppelin's "Stairway to Heaven" wafted through the sweet blue haze that had fogged the car's interior. Although Mom was no fan of rock music, she nonetheless said, "Turn that up. I like that song." After a time, Mom complained, "I'm not really feeling anything from this thing." She paused, then said, "Hey! There's a 7-Eleven. Pull over. I want a Snicker Bar!"

Our youngest sibling shared this memory:

Mom was always my buffer between Dad. From my childhood into adulthood, she knew how hard Dad could be, so she interceded on many occasions that Dad would have overreacted to. She had a way of looking out for me. I was her baby. Mom was more carefree, always pleasant, always being a mom. Mom was always lighthearted and cheery when I had friends over. She loved my friends and they loved her.

On one occasion Mom and I went to Playhouse Square and saw Pearl Bailey at the Palace Theater. We both dressed up, and I drove her car downtown and we had a 'date.' It was my college freshman summer. I was not sure what to expect of an evening with one of her favorite performers. I was used to rock concerts and sporting events. Let me tell you, IT WAS AWESOME!

Mom told me about Pearl Bailey's drummer, Eddie Belson, who was also her husband. She was a "big ole girl," as Mom put it, and Eddie was a small white dude. Their marriage was rather scandalous in the day. Boy, could that guy drum. Move over Buddy Rich.

I could not believe how much fun we had, sharing her music. I actually pursued seeing some of the old time performers from Mom and Dad's era afterward. Thanks for the great date, Mom.

I am thinking of her and all of the fun we had. She was a great mom to me.

This is from a letter Mom wrote to a sister-in-law about the "unique qualities" of her children. "Of course, they are extra special to us. Although they didn't exactly fall into the molds envisioned by us, they really make us proud of them."

On December 23, 1977, one of her youngest sons was killed in a car accident. I was twenty-nine at the time and incapable then and now of fathoming the full depth of grief that accompanies the loss of one's child. After the funeral, the rest of us returned to our lives, and Mom retreated to her upstairs bedroom. According to the youngest in the family who was still living at home, for the next two months, she rarely changed out of her pajamas and only came downstairs occasionally to get food. "Dad held it all together during this horrible time."

When I sent the following letter to my mother in April 1995, lung cancer, probably caused by decades of smoking, and the 105 radiation treatments she endured that scarred her little body from the inside out, had robbed her of her indomitable energy and keen wit.

Dear Mom,

I tell you all the time that I think of you. It's true. I've mentioned that I'm trying to be more aware of life on a moment-to-moment basis. I'm trying to slow down and savor the blessings of life, to reorient more towards people and less towards accomplishments. This is not new for me. I've been trying for a long time but only with marginal progress.

Well, I mention this because you're a big part of this. When I pause during the day and take a calming breath or two to "center," so often you are there. I wonder how you are feeling, if you are getting better, worse, or just still "hanging on." This has to be the most difficult thing you have ever experienced. It must be hard to bolster hope that things will get better when your health doesn't actually comply with your wishes. Do you fear dying or death? Do you think back and re-evaluate life?

I know I'm projecting my own questions. I'm guessing that how I might feel is the way you might feel. Maybe I'm wrong.

As I sat quietly and thought this morning, I traced the person I am today back to the two people who had the greatest influence on me—you and Dad. I can pick out periods that seem diverse (child, seminarian, soldier, deckhand, hippy radical, vagabond, husband, parent, guitar player, city planner, etc.) but at my core, I haven't really changed since you raised me. I have long recognized that the set of fundamental values that you both instilled in me has been my keel throughout life.

Over the years, we have disagreed about the particulars how these values get played out in the world. No surprise there. If there were easy answers in life, life's problems would be long solved. More importantly, the ethical foundation you both gave me propelled me towards the seminary. What I learned and experienced there has been invaluable to me my whole life. I compromised my ethics by going to Vietnam, which is why that experience has been so hard for me. But I found my course again, learned from the experience—plus the priceless lesson of a bad marriage—and now have the joy of twenty-two years with Cynthia and Jessica. Thank you for starting me on this course.

When I look at Jessica, I see this same thing. I still see the little girl that Cynthia and I raised. I sang the same "Cotton Fields" song to her that you sang to me as a child. I know her happiness, her fears, her weaknesses, her creativity and skills, her innate goodness, and her inner peace. When she is troubled, I remember her child's version of the same thing. When she makes life choices in sync with my values, I know she is not doing it to please me. She's doing it because it's a reflection of the values Cynthia and I raised her with. Your influence lives on to future generations.

Sometime, I would like to talk with you about this more, Mom. I know I've said many of these things before and we have talked about them, but important things are worth repeating.

I love you.

Although she loved to pen articulate letters in a lovely handwriting that befit the beauty she surrounded herself with all of her life, she couldn't muster the energy to reply to my letter, even by phone. She died six weeks later at home, surrounded by family.

Cynthia And Jessica

"You are a very fortunate person, Michael, to have a spouse so wise and loving, so strong, yet so patient as Cynthia." When he made this comment, I had been telling Thomas about a letter she had recently found buried in her computer from ten years earlier. Also buried in the complex interplay of relationships among my immediate family members was my cowardice and guilt for rarely defending Cynthia from my father's insults and Jessica from his neglect as a grandparent.

Cynthia has the skill of a prize fighter in retorts. When Dad would slide a subtle insult under my rusty radar, Cynthia would instantly rise to our defense before I could even begin my characteristic regression back to my little boy timidity. Dad had so imprinted me with the duty to listen that I preferred retreat so that Cynthia could engage in verbal battle with him while I rationalized that she would always do better than I ever could. She won every battle but at great cost to her. "Why didn't you say something?" I never had an adequate answer for her, or myself.

The letter Cynthia rediscovered illustrates how hard she tried for decades to maintain a positive relationship with my parents. With Sisyphean determination, she tried to help fill the relationship vacuum I had with my parents. She dogged me to call on a regular basis; we drove the 737 miles to Cleveland about every nine months; she never failed to send cards and gifts for every occasion Hallmark marketed. She even tried to bridge the gulf of silence about my experience in Vietnam a decade before I was willing to deal with it with Thomas. Here's an excerpt from her letter addressed to both of my parents that illustrates the point:

Last weekend we went to see a performance that a friend produced. She was hired by a coalition of churches and groups to write (and perform) a play on "gender equity."

She had interviewed several people and wove their stories into a very creative presentation using acting and song. As it turned out, the male actor's character was based on our own Michael. It was weird seeing an actor ("William" in the play) tell one of Michael's stories—our "pilgrimage," as Michael calls it, to the Vietnam Veterans Memorial Wall. Jessica was eighteen at the time. I had suggested that Jessica and Michael stand at either end of the panels that listed the dead during Michael's tour of duty—March 1969 to March 1970, so I could snap a picture of that year of death. The black polished granite panels, numbers thirteen to thirty-one, towered well beyond the reach of Michael's hand. That year engulfed a major portion of the monument's inscriptions.

The character, William, told the story slowly with all the details Michael had related to our friend. He described how he (Michael) would tell his daughter "Lucy" (Jessica) to "just cope" when she was having trouble with friends or situations in high school. Then he talked about going to the Wall and looking up the name of a friend he served with, John Kitsen. A land mine killed John five days after his nineteenth birthday, a little over four months after he and Michael had arrived in Vietnam. William described in lovely detail how the names on the Wall looked like a black lake and how the wall reflected the images of all who stood before it as he looked for John's name.

When he found the name and started to take a rubbing of it, letter by letter, "J ... O ... H . . ." emerged and he broke down completely. His daughter comforted him and he discovered it wasn't that easy to "just cope with it." Later, he realized that this was a moment when he was a good father. He had connected with his daughter and allowed her to see his vulnerability. Many people in the audience wept when they heard this story, but none harder than the three of us. It was a very moving and strange experience watching a piece of our life played out on a stage before us.

Jessica was thirty one when I started therapy. In the same way that my father had limited ability to raise me with sufficient attention and unconditional love, I have to believe the same is true at least to some degree for the father who helped raise Jessica. No doubt, through the countervailing influence of her mother, Jessica matured into a compassionate, wise, and loving person despite my drug of choice during her childhood—work-aholism, and the trickle-down trauma that Cynthia wrote about so eloquently in her book, *Shock Waves.*

Today, as the mother of fifteen-year-old twin boys, she maintains an amazing devotion to the wellbeing of her family while balancing her professional career as a writer.

PART III

*The First Trauma Informs
the Second*

Prelude: Caution in the Waking

Waking Him

Careful not to startle him,
She tip-toes into the room and watches. His eyes
Are squeezed shut and twitch slightly
With the intensity of his sleep.

Quietly, she calls him
"Daddy . . . Daddy are you sleeping?"
She has learned to wake him slowly.
If she is too sudden, he will uncoil
A fierce spring rusted loose.

Gently, she must nudge him back
Into the world of fenced-in yards
And refrigerator art, away
From the shadowy echoes of rotten canvas and death.

She knows her child hand is not enough,
Because even she is in some of those dreams.
Staggering with him shoeless through mud.
That is all he will say. He tries
To protect her, but she hears
The screams at night. She already knows.

She must use caution in the waking.

Dreams

She watches me sleep.
I know this, and I know
She approaches me with the heart
Of a bird that flutters
More than it beats.
And I know this is because
She is afraid (must be afraid)

Of my sleep.

I know this because she is there
with me sometimes,
staggering through the mud and confusion.
There is no safe place,
No way to escape the smell and the death,
Or the quiet in my right ear.

With her I am NEVER angry, because
With the heart of a bird
She is afraid of my sleep.[19]

—Jessica A. Orange

7. NAMING PTSD AND ITS EFFECTS

Severe trauma explodes the cohesion of consciousness. When a survivor creates fully realized narrative that brings together the shattered knowledge of what happened, the emotions that were aroused by the meaning of the events, and the bodily sensations that the physical events created, the survivor pieces back together the fragmentation of consciousness that trauma caused. Such narrative often results in the remission of some symptoms ... . Narrative enables the survivor to rebuild the ruins of character.
—Jonathan Shay, *Achilles in Vietnam*

It is not by moving rocks that we find happiness and awakening, but by transforming our relationship with them.
—Jack Kornfield, *A Path with Heart*

I tell Thomas the stories of trying to determine the body count from body parts in free-fire zones and the trembling giddiness after surviving a firefight. The ethereal beauty of the countryside viewed at sunrise from the ramp's edge of a Sea Knight chopper flying at treetop level into the Que Son mountains. I try to describe the distinct sound of individual bones slowly breaking in an old Vietnamese man, and the smell of gunpowder smoke and burning skin and hair. I struggle to explain how I could passively watch, frozen in the thick red Vietnamese mud, while my unit tortured two teenage boys with cigarettes. Time after time, we re-open infected emotional wounds in Thomas's hospital for the soul.

After six months, Thomas and I agreed it was time to revisit the issues born in Vietnam and to integrate them with what I had learned about my childhood. Trauma caused by war fit within my youthful sense of traditional maleness. The gravitas of combat provided sufficient grounds to be screwed up a bit. In other words, it was marginally macho. On the other hand, to be bothered all these years by childhood issues that I had minimized seemed, before therapy … well, childish. This idea of the "manliness" of war and its effects is, of course, ageless, but for us Vietnam vets, there were other complicating factors. As Terrence Real puts it, "Until Vietnam vets demanded the medical sector [deal with their PTSD], society blamed soldiers for their weakness, for their unmanliness and cowardice—a double injury." The hard work on the original childhood trauma prepared me to next extend compassion to the twenty-year-old soldier, the "tender-hearted boy," as Thomas called him.

Too many times after these early morning sessions I found myself paralyzed in the parking lot near my workplace with embarrassing sobs rocking the car. Too many times, I fled back home into Cynthia's loving arms instead of shuffling to the office like a prisoner on death row. Spurred by Cynthia's concern and prodding, I sought an unpaid leave of absence from my employer. Thomas submitted a letter on my behalf recommending an extended medical leave of three to six months so that I could deal with the PTSD and to prevent a "physical and/or emotional breakdown." My primary physician also made this case in support of me. The director agreed, and I made my last three months of therapy my full-time job.

There's power in naming.

An important milestone for me came during my crash

after President Bush invaded Iraq when I finally realized that I needed an outside authority to tell me whether I had PTSD. I wanted a diagnosis—yes or no. Soon after starting therapy with Thomas, I discovered it helped tremendously to learn that what I had experienced for so long was an identifiable *disorder* (the D in PTSD) with a course of treatment. I no longer had to fumble along on my own trying to figure things out indirectly by studying the history of the Vietnam War and the effects of soldiering through books, university courses, and movies. There were answers out there and experts to help. The same was true for my exploration of the effects of childhood neglect.

Having come to know me deeply by the last month of my therapy, Thomas said that I probably would have come to grips with the effects of my childhood trauma decades ago were it not for the subsequent trauma and PTSD from Vietnam. "At thirteen," he said, "you sensed your need to escape your dysfunctional family when you left home to live in the seminary and find other father figures to meet your needs. You never moved back to that home environment after that, so you were on a healthy path. But Vietnam and the PTSD it caused robbed you of that fuller, more genuine life."

He explained that the degree of PTSD was too great for me to face until, first, the price it exacted became intolerable; and second, I was finally ready to confront it and accept treatment. Thomas then helped me develop the tools I needed to cope with the depression and other effects associated with both the childhood issues and the PTSD.

"Bizarro World" Therapy

I remember confessing to Cynthia that therapy was making me feel more like a woman. We laughed and talked more about it, and then I revised my statement to "I'm feeling more like a human; more complete and authentic." I drew up the following list to summarize some of the key lessons of my therapy. It reminded me of the Bizarro World in the Superman comics where things are the opposite of normal.

Prior Values	"Bizarro World" Therapy Values
Suppress "feminine" feelings, control anger, and act manly, courageously, and decisively.	Reconnect with all feelings and "own" them. Be compassionate with the "feeling" inner child.
Bury painful childhood memories and cover it over with a positive spin. Be a Pollyanna.	Gauge the damage done from the child's perspective. Link that damage to the responsible adults but bring understanding and compassion as to the reasons for their actions.
Foster a forward focus and drive.	Slow down, do less, and enjoy the moment.
Be optimistic; focus on the good in everything.	Be realistic.
Set high personal standards.	Set realistic personal standards and avoid "moral superiority."
Seek "atta-boys" through accomplishments of body, mind, and spirit.	Foster a healthy self-esteem and find meaning less through doing and more through being.

Retreat—I Have Arrived I Am Home [20]

Pre-dawn dew soaked through my sandals as I took the more direct route from the campground to the meditation hall across a wide field of grass. A playful déjà vu sensation enveloped me as I recalled cutting across yards and fields as a child in contrast to my adult habit of staying to the sidewalks. The low croak of frogs and the songs from birds and crickets welcomed me. As I neared a tree line, the glorious halleluiah chorus of mating songs from cicadas looking for love after their seventeen-year sojourn underground reminded me of my longtime love of their calls and amazement of their life cycle. Funny how my Vietnam experiences resulted in a constant ringing in both ears that most resembles a cicada's song.

A police official in Madison, Wisconsin had organized this five-day retreat at the nearby Green Lake resort in August 2003 with the hope that police officers and others in public service would attend. The moment I heard of it and that Thich Nhat Hạnh, the Vietnamese Buddhist monk I so respected, would lead it, I felt drawn to be with a spiritual leader from the war-torn country that was the source of my moral injuries.

My tour of duty in Vietnam produced a case of post-traumatic stress disorder (PTSD) that I now know is very typical for combat vets. At the time of the retreat, I was in my fourth month of weekly talk therapy sessions with Thomas and by then the VA had agreed that I was partially disabled due to combat-induced PTSD.

I walked across the field that first morning towards the meditation hall to join the other retreatants in a walking meditation. Still enveloped by the "Noble Silence" that began at 7:30 the night before, the crowd shifted attention when Thich Nhat Hạnh (or *Thay*, "teacher" in Vietnamese), joined the gathering, followed by his entourage of monks and nuns. A monk "invited a bell to sound." First, he gave it two deliberate strokes muted by his palm, paused, and then struck a solid resonating chime that embraced the assembly. Thay began the walk.

We turned toward Green Lake and the sun lit the lake's low fog with a rosy hue. I savored the feel of the breeze and the unevenness of the rocky path. A musky smell wafted off the cattails and an egret stalked the shoreline. A profound silence reigned as five hundred people mindfully walked. I planted the heel of my foot, slowly shifted my weight over it, and then brought my other heel down a few inches further down the trail as I breathed in rhythm with this methodical pace. Thay had hit the mute switch on life's remote, quieting the memories and ghosts that so often invaded my thoughts and dreams.

Two days later, I decided to go directly to the lake and discreetly take pictures of the walking meditation. I settled on a spot where the shoreline jutted out a few feet. Like a thousand-legged millipede, Thay led everyone towards my perch. Until this moment, the closest I had been to this world-famous man was about sixty feet. He floated in and out of the meditation hall for his dharma talks, but other than the walking meditation, we never saw him. I learned that a stomach ailment had long plagued him with near constant pain, limiting his activities.

I felt a little sheepish. Although I planned on joining the walk after the main body had passed behind me, I worried that Thay and anyone else who might see me would think I shouldn't be acting as retreat paparazzi. Instead, Thay walked ten feet beyond me, turned towards the sunrise, and sat down. In a few seconds everyone else did the same. The holy man was so close I was able subtly to snap a photo that captured both the age of the man and the deep serenity nurtured by a life of meditation and good works—an image I shall always treasure.

I sank into my own meditation. The radiance of the sun penetrated my shut lids. Someone a few feet behind me began to play a flute. Tears came, not from the sadness that I was trying so hard to contain but from the sheer joy in the beauty of it all.

Later, we returned to the meditation hall for Thay's dharma talk, and I did my best to fold my legs under me and

EMBRACING THE GHOST 177

rekindle Thay's lesson of mindfulness. A large banner on the wall to my left read, "i have arrived i am home." I wondered if the lower case "i" was to remind us of the ego's link to craving and the Buddha's lesson that grasping is the source of suffering.

In slow motion, Thay poured water into a glass, moved it two-handed to his lips, and smelled it before he sipped. Light twinkled from his smile off a silver-coated tooth. With a soft voice muffled by a thick Vietnamese accent, he advised that mindful observation is the "element which nourishes the tree of understanding, and compassion and love are the most beautiful flowers."

He paused and took another slow sip of water. "A beautiful meditation practice is to picture yourself when you were a five-year-old." Then, after a time, he asked us to do the same for our parents and then their parents. He said the suggestion concerned the continuity of life and was a technique to be compassionate for the childhood of your parents. "Your parents and ancestors are in you and you are in your children." He referenced the nature of family problems being passed down from generation to generation. "Like you, your father as a boy may have been the victim of his father." I know he is right. So often I hear my father's gruff voice come from my mouth as I age. His adages are increasingly becoming more valuable as my memory fades.

Only one other retreat leader garnered comparable respect: Sister Chan Khong. She had been an ordained co-leader with Thay in the Southeast Asian relief efforts for refugees and war victims since the 1960s. The smooth skin of her face and near constant smile did not betray the psychic scars a decade of war surely inflicted on her. She sang us into meditation several times with her high lilting voice, and closed one day with a beautiful French lullaby, alternating the verses in French, Vietnamese, and English.

Another morning, she guided us through a total relaxation exercise and then asked us to first stand and consider the positive attributes of our parents, and then lay face down and consider their negative attributes. We repeated the exercise considering the positive and negative aspects of our ancestors, our hometown and, finally, our country. The American mythology of my childhood education served for my consideration of my country's positive attributes, and my experiences in Vietnam for the negative.

Towards the end of the retreat, we were invited to submit a written request and reason for a consultation with a nun or priest. I submitted a request stating my struggle with PTSD. Sister Chan Khong chose me.

I didn't know how to start and she suggested with a soft reassuring voice, "Start with the worst." I struggled with an instantly dry mouth and got out only three words: "We killed children..." I choked on my tears as my face scrunched. I told her an abbreviated version of one war story—my first experience with the atrocity that is war. I took a breath and told her the tower story.

After a long pause, Sister Khong said that if I practiced mindfulness, I could look deeply into the nature of myself and touch my suffering. I could learn to live with my fear, my doubts, my confusion, my guilt, and my anger. My task, she said, was to dwell in those places like still water, but if I didn't practice mindfulness, I would continue to live in forgetfulness, controlled by my suffering.

She shared a war story that had bothered her for years about a village west of Saigon that was trapped by minefields, blown bridges and impassable roads. She decided to bring the village much-needed food and medical supplies by boat up the Mekong River, but fighting was raging on both sides of the river. She trusted that the neutrality of the boat's Buddhist flag would pause the fighting long enough for her boat to pass.

As she approached the village, a woman came running to her holding her bleeding baby. "She gave me the baby and said, 'Please save my baby.'" While Sister Khong made her way back to the boat for medical supplies, she felt the baby lurch; it gave out a sigh, and died. It was crushing, she said, to hand the baby back to the wailing mother. "There was so much death. So many bombs." So many children lost to war, I thought. We were two combat vets sharing stories, sharing grief.

She asked me if I brought something home from Vietnam that was beautiful. The only thing I could think of was the photo of Mai Lee, a young girl I had befriended. She said, "Think of her when these feelings come back." She offered a final suggestion: "I try to give joy to one person in the morning and reduce the suffering of one person in the afternoon by deep listening; deep compassion."

I thanked the kindly nun. Like the initial sensation in an elevator going down, the gravity of my past had less of a drag on me.

Thirty-three years after the war, I began to feel like i had arrived. i was home.

Final Trip Up The Tower

I feel compelled to return one last time to the tower story, the one Thomas used repeatedly to help me foster compassion. Compassion for the dead boys, for their parents and the people of Vietnam, and especially for the young Marine who was the closest to the slaughter but who stayed above the fray, quivering with his finger poised on his un-pulled trigger. Thomas suggested I "unpack" the story once more by unveiling the insights gleaned from my therapy; the things I learned since I first wrote the story down in 1996.

The birth of our identical twin grandsons in 2006 initiated profound changes in Cynthia and my life together. We had the opportunity to stay with them for weeks at a time in Colorado during their first two years and we have retained a treasured closeness after they moved less than an hour away here in St. Paul. Grandfathering became a pathway to my reaching a level of emotional maturity that made me receptive to the rarity and importance of this gift.[21]

Many times, I've sensed an overwhelming need to protect them from all harm. It's a dark fear that I feel compelled to describe so that I can come to understand it and integrate it. The ties within our two families are so intense. Disturbing thoughts of loss invade my loving spirit; thoughts that, somehow, something will disrupt this precious period of my life, that something will sever these ties. It has no specificity or name, but it lurks nonetheless and makes me feel vulnerable. Perhaps it's a residue from my staid Catholic upbringing that instilled me with the notion of unworthiness; that there's a dark cloud within every silver lining.

My ghosts from Vietnam haunt me still because I know my bullets and shells gave specificity and name to tragedy there. It took me fifteen years to gather the strength and wisdom to be able to admit publicly that I killed people in that war. It doesn't matter that they were somewhere in the distance and I couldn't see bodies fall when the mortar rounds struck. War kills, and as a combat soldier, I was complicit in the carnage. It has taken this grandfathering experience to be capable of fathoming the grief my shells blasted out of peoples' lives, and relationships too. Relationships among spouses, parents, children, brothers, and sisters—and grandparents.

The tower experience showed the twenty-year-old Marine how war destroys people, but he was too young to grasp its full significance beyond passively absorbing the shocks deep into his marrow like a dangerous dose of radioactivity. Therapy showed the middle-aged man the depth of his own personal loss. But it was the twins who showed their grandfather the essence of unconditional love and made him capable of imagining its companion risk, the bone-crushing anguish that the loss of a child would cause. With this comes the deep compassion that is the core lesson of the tower story.

PART IV

The End Is the Beginning

Prelude: Giving Back the Tears

I remember the day when I felt Michael and I had truly
gained entrance into the "great family of the heavy-
hearted." It was September 26, 1992—the dedication of
the Minnesota Vietnam Veterans Memorial. Prior to that
day, our journey through trauma and tears had—for the
most part—been an intimate one. Michael was becoming more open about his combat experience, but we
hadn't yet uncovered how far-reaching was the poison
of war.

We approached that day and the dedication tentatively, fearing it would be more a platform for politicians
than a solemn honoring of the soldiers who died in
the service of their country. Yet we were hopeful. We
knew of the memorial's history; how volunteers worked
diligently for four years to raise money on their own
because most corporations and organizations still considered Vietnam too controversial; how the stalled project only came back to life when Sally Adams—mother
of a shattered Vietnam veteran and grandmother—
climbed up a 25-foot billboard and vowed to stay there
until the last funds were raised. She came down after
three weeks, and work on the memorial began.

We were also curious. We got wind that other veterans who evidently shared our apprehensions had arranged for a Native American spiritual elder to come
early, before the public event, for a private, "Giving Back
the Tears" ceremony.

Michael and I held hands tightly as we walked across
the granite map of Indochina, down the winding concrete path that connects it to a map of Minnesota, com-
prised of 68,000 granite squares, one for each Minneso-
tan who served in Vietnam. Of those squares, 1,120 are
dark green for those who did not return—whose names

are also carved on the granite wall that hugs the plaza. To one side is a pool of water to symbolize Minnesota's many lakes, and a small limestone house to represent the idea of coming home.

About twenty veterans and loved ones stood silently in this sacred space as the elder in ceremonial dress used an eagle feather to waft sage smoke over each of us. His native chants were rhythmic and soothing, a soft blessing. He lit an intricately carved peace pipe and offered it to each of us. In the distance, we heard drums, faint at first but growing stronger and more pronounced as we completed the ritual. When the holy man began moving to the drum's heartbeat, we followed. My feet felt heavy and awkward at first, but became lighter as he led us from the granite plaza to the soft and welcoming grass. It was a dance of mourning. I soon lost myself in the experience. My plodding feet and heavy heart becoming one with the drum.

When the drum grew slower and quieter, the elder stopped to sit on a chair by a bucket of clear water that held a long-handled ladle. One by one, he motioned for each of us to approach, and, as we did, he scooped some cool water and held the ladle to our mouths. He urged us to give our tears to the earth as we replenished ourselves with pure, shared water. It was a soldiers' communion; a fellowship of the heavy-hearted; a benediction for the broken.

Earth to earth. As our tears mingled and fell together to the ground, I imagined them nourishing the soil, giving life to future greenness. As I stood by these wounded warriors, clinging to the husband I so fiercely loved, I was filled with gratitude and hope. We were still standing. We were standing together.[22]

—Cynthia Orange

8. TEAR BY TEAR

There is a sacredness in tears. They are not the mark of weakness, but of power. They speak more eloquently than ten thousand tongues. They are the messengers of overwhelming grief, of deep contrition, and of unspeakable love.

—Washington Irving

When it seems that our sorrow is too great to be borne, let us think of the great family of the heavy-hearted into which our grief has given us entrance, and inevitably, we will feel about us, their arms and their understanding.

—Helen Keller

Lest I leave the impression that I'm cured of PTSD or that there is a cure, I must point out that I have had a couple of serious but short-lived relapses since completing therapy in January 2004 and have revisited Thomas several times since then. Also, I have been a member of two PTSD groups and I have redirected my compulsive energy primarily to veterans' causes. "Paying it forward," I find fulfillment in trying to share what I have learned with others, which is a primary reason for writing this book.

Imbedded in the word *re-cover* is the implication that covering over emotional experiences again is a good thing. We need a better word. I suggest *embrace*. A friend with PTSD told me about the advice of the group therapist at the VA who uses driving a bus as a metaphor for living. "Don't turn around, just keep driving; and, whatever you do, don't get off the bus." The patients are not to figuratively turn around because behind them riding on the bus are the ghosts that are their PTSD sources. "Getting off the bus" is code for suicide. Based on my therapy, I'd give very different advice. I'd tell them to stop the bus and not start again until they had gotten to know every one of their ghosts and embraced them as their teachers.

Claude Anshin Thomas confirms this advice in his book, *At Hell's Gate: A Soldier's Journey from War to Peace*: "Healing is not the absence of suffering. What happens is that through this process of being more present to my own life, I stop attempting to reject suffering. This is healing and transformation ... . I breathe in and breathe out, and I am grateful to be free to touch these emotions, to establish a different relationship with them, to be able to have the possibility to make different choices in my life. When I live in forgetfulness, I have no choice. My conditioned nature is deciding for me ... . But trapped in forgetfulness, we cannot resist clinging to our desires ... and to our conditioning ... and so we remain trapped in an endless cycle of suffering, repeating the dynamic again and again."

Work was never the same after my crash in 2003. When I first walked into my office after my three-month medical leave of absence, it felt like a place preserved as a museum for a life I no longer lived there. Getting healthier tempered my workaholism. I no longer needed it as a diversion. My overall happiness increased as I became less obsessed. On the other hand, my ability to perform at work depended on my workaholic drive. With diminished compulsivity, I struggled unsuccessfully to maintain my normal energy level, commitment, and workload. When I was eligible for retirement two difficult years later, I changed my lifelong intention to work until the day I dropped dead. With perfect timing, my retirement party was one week after our daughter gave birth to the twins. I'm very good at my new job, grandfathering. It's the most fulfilling job I've ever had.

Thomas asked if there was a key thing that would keep me on track. It was the easiest question he'd asked. "Cynthia," I said; "My relationship with Cynthia." More important than Thomas, Thich Nhat Hahn, the books I read, and all of the friends and family who helped me, were the decades of non-judgmental love, patience, compassion, and acceptance from Jessica and especially Cynthia. She has stood by me since 1973 when we married. With saint-like patience and wisdom, she listened intently to my descriptions of every one of my forty-four sessions with Thomas. She has a gift. With silence—almost stillness—she drew me out before I learned how much she saw all along. She anticipated my needs, served as my advocate for my medical leave of absence, and offered her wisdom and love as the healing balm for my wounds and inadequacies. For every hour I spent in a chair opposite Thomas in his office, I spent one or more at home opposite Cynthia sharing the experience of my therapy, my reading, and my writing.

The tremendous burden of it all for Cynthia far outweighed the sum of the hours spent listening, absorbing, sorting, remembering, suggesting, and controlling her own emotional reactions. There is a special burden of *carrying the whole*, as one friend put it. Thomas invested the time in his therapy office and the time between my visits that he spent on my case, and family and friends donated many hours listening to me and sharing their concern for me. But for Cynthia, my therapy and my PTSD was an unwelcome presence that crowded our relationship. The default setting of my brain when it wasn't engaged in something else was PTSD, therapy, and writing, which generated a primordial low rumble that vibrated beneath my thoughts and dreams. It was a toothache that refused to recede into the background noise of everyday pains. She never complained although I'm sure compassion fatigue was very real for her. She was always there. Like an alchemist, she continues to help me transform the poison of war into an alloy that makes me stronger; that makes us stronger.

As Mother Teresa put it, "Love cannot remain by itself—it has no meaning. Love has to be put into action and that action is service." The great spiritual teachers agree that enlightenment is possible for everyone and that living a life of good works is evidence of having reached some degree of enlightenment. That's my Cynthia.

I could have been drawn down the same suicidal path my friends Chris and Leo took but Cynthia and Jessica, along with our many family members and friends, opened their arms to me with a loving kindness that keeps me on the path through the rich life I'm living. After nearly five decades of marriage, during which she bore the brunt of my PTSD symptoms, she had the incredible patience to hold my hand every step of the way as I waded back through the jungle muck; the exploded bodies; and the betrayals by parents, church, and country. I know it was exhausting work for her.

Before therapy, she was there for me as my writing teacher, my editor, and my lay therapist during the five years it took me to write my first book. I like to say her fingerprints are on every page. How much attention to her friends, interests, and work did my first priority status displace?

PTSD poses serious tests to a relationship. It can drive wedges among partners, parents, and children. My PTSD was the main reason Cynthia began her own course of talk therapy. Since PTSD suppresses feelings and thrives on compulsions and distractions, I know it made me much less accessible and empathetic, and it severely compromised my ability and willingness to be a good father and husband. I was both too present (when I needed her) and too distant (when I was obsessing on therapy—and PTSD before then).

Cynthia and Jessica paid a high price. Considering all of the attention we pay to honor the sacrifices of our soldiers and veterans, why is there no national holiday or marble monument to commemorate their loved ones who help repair the damage and who cope with the loss?

For Cynthia and me, our courses of therapy made us

stronger and more committed to our marriage. Our struggles have informed our lives and opened us up to more compassion for others. My reanimated feelings help me honor the pain of my past trauma, and simultaneously be present and open to today's opportunities for joy and serenity.

Thomas said it well, "Cynthia's such an important person for you, helping you home finally from Vietnam, tear by tear."

9. FOUR TOOLS OF RECOVERY

A year ago, the mid-August temperature topped a hundred degrees in St. Paul but the evening's deluge relieved the atmosphere's pent up energy. I donned my poncho and settled in on a lawn chair in the middle of our backyard patio. The rain splashed into the night's second brandy.

The splatter echoing within my hood triggered a flood of emotive memories of nights on patrol. I vividly recalled the exhaustion of humping 65 pounds of gear and rounds through tropical heat so stifling I could feel sweat boil out of my skin. How sweat couldn't cool; it could only salt the meal for the mosquitoes and flies. How the smell of my rotting feet matched what oozed from feted paddy muck. How the foxhole I carved out of Vietnam's red soil was just large enough for a cross-legged crouch with my M16 across my lap. How the memories never fade.

A Minnesota thunderstorm is no match for Vietnam's. The roar of a Vietnam downpour could drown out all but a shout between our perimeter foxholes.

Sitting in a comfortable chair within the security of my back yard patio, a shiver coursed down from my shoulders and I recalled the bone-rattling cold of nights sitting half-submerged in a hole while on search-and-destroy missions. Two hours on guard, then two hours of coma-like sleep, then repeat until sunrise. Then start over the next night. But I knew that my enemy had it worse and that the rain made attack unlikely. An uncomfortable protector.

I finished my brandy and came inside to my loving wife's acceptance of my befuddling behaviors, profoundly appreciative of the preciousness of my life and the opportunity to love and be loved.

Heart Work—The First Tool Of Recovery

Looking back, I can see four tools that are important for my ongoing recovery. The first primary tool for my recovery was the "heart work" of finding compassion for myself first as a child and then as a young soldier. During my therapy, I began to observe boys of that critical age for me, eight to ten years old. At downtown bus stops, shopping centers, and city streets I saw parents holding their children's hands with love and protection on their faces. I also saw children yanked into compliance and harshly criticized and shamed. I saw the look of pain on their impressionable faces. The lesson I took away was to appreciate the profound innocence and helplessness of the child as compared to the god-like power of the parent. These observations helped me view my childhood experiences through the eyes of the child that was affected by them, not the fifty-five-year-old in therapy. Only then was I able to appreciate how the environment my siblings and I experienced as kids could have had lasting effects through adulthood. I applied this same approach to my war experiences.

So many times, I heard people (other than Cynthia and the wisest members of my family and friends) tell me to just get over it and put the war and the bad feelings behind me and move on. Through therapy, I learned that there is a lot of projection associated with suffering. We think that people or things outside ourselves are the cause of our suffering or that something outside us heals us—a physician, a therapist, a preacher, or a miracle from God. I accept the Buddhist perspective that we are responsible for our own healing. We need tools to help us on our path and they are all rooted in spiritual practice, rooted in the truth that we cannot hide our suffering or eradicate it. I accepted that Vietnam has consequences in my life. I needed to learn how to embrace the suffering from that war so that I could spot it when it crept up and threatened to control my life. When it arrives, it is up to me to choose how to act in relation to it. The decision is mine.

Headwork—The Second Tool Of Recovery

My therapy included both heart work and even more head-work (a friend said to me, "Michael, you think your way to your feelings"). The second major tool for my recovery involved understanding my childhood intellectually. My passport to com-prehension during therapy was the book Thomas recommended that I've cited frequently in this writing, *I Don't Want to Talk About It*, by Terrence Real. Real's book focused on the father-son relationship, and as I said, for me, the parent who, by far, had the most significant effect was my father.

Perhaps the adage "like father, like son" best summarizes it. With scientific precision, Real describes the psychological underpinnings why and how a father who was abused by his father can pass that same abuse on to his son in a trickle-down fashion. Real described my family perfectly. He wrote that the key component of a boy's healthy relationship to his father is affection, not "masculinity." Boys who fare poorly in their psychological adjustment are not those without fathers, he ex-plained, but those with abusive or neglectful fathers. "Boys don't hunger for fathers who will model masculinity. They hunger for fathers who will rescue them from it. They need fathers who have themselves emerged from the gauntlet of their own socialization with some degree of emotional intactness. Sons don't want their fathers' 'balls;' they want their hearts … . What we give our boys is performance-based esteem, not an essential sense of worth that comes from within. One cannot earn self-esteem. One has it. Performance-based esteem augments an in-sufficient sense of worth by the measuring of one's accomplish-ments against those of others, and coming out on top."

Since PTSD is a form of depression, I paid close attention to Real's description of the process where kids take on their par-ents' problems; their alcoholism, shame, low self-esteem, rage, and self-hate. I locked away the part of me that was damaged by my parents' toxic problems and parenting and then built up defenses to insulate and protect myself. The optimistic attitude I maintained, which ran on my positive spin on my childhood, was one of my most important defenses. I was a positivity junkie. With Thomas's help, I took on the task of re-parenting myself.

Human brain evolution biases us towards negativity. In his book, *Buddha's Brain: The Practical Neuroscience of Happiness, Love & Wisdom*, Dr. Rick Hanson describes how our early mammalian ancestors dealt with the sticks and carrots of survival. He wrote that paying more attention to the sticks (threats and suffering) as opposed to the carrots (the chance of a meal or to mate) resulted in better chances of survival. "The ones that lived to pass on their genes paid a *lot* of attention to negative experiences." He cites a study that demonstrated that generally it takes about five positive interactions in a relationship to overcome a single negative one.

My *headwork* led to a better understanding of the parent-child relationship, which, in turn, sparked compassion for my parents and other parents who could not be expected to parent in a language they could not speak. (The Appendix and Resources sections at the end contains additional information from these wise authors.)

Owning Anger And Embracing Shame—The Third Tool Of Recovery

As I mentioned, I realized that I joined the service and went to Vietnam to say a big "screw you" to my parents, and especially to my father. I thought, out of anger and frustration, if I survived, maybe that would win my father's love and acceptance; and if I died, it would punish him in some way. It was a pseudo-suicide attempt. Thomas commented on the significance of this matter, "You were so angry, you could kill—it could be VC or by getting yourself killed."

I think part of why the death of the two boys in the tower story has such a profound effect on me is that I hold deep compassion for children who have been betrayed by their parents. The third key tool for my ongoing recovery required a more genuine sensing, owning, and expressing of my anger; a task that was very difficult for me.

During my retreat, Thich Nhat Hanh talked a lot about anger. He said that anger is a shield for grief and that there is cord that connects the anger and grief back to a prior hurt—what Cynthia refers to as "the story behind the story." The practice of expressing anger, Thay warned, is not a venting but just that, a practice that waters the seed of anger, which will lead to more sorrow. "I am my anger. I own it, and I should embrace it with mindfulness and tenderness to gain understanding about its roots," he advised. He said that this practice does not lead to expressing the anger nor repressing it, but rather transforming it. "If a baby cries, the mother goes to it and deals with the source of the problem. She does not suppress the crying. We should do the same with the 'baby' of our anger. Holding it tenderly may be all that is needed."

Thomas offered a slightly different approach from this wise monk's advice. He said that PTSD relies on powerlessness. He suggested I get to know and appreciate my anger and its power, authority, and authenticity. Claim it: "I'm feeling anger." He said there was a beast inside me like the ones that howl in the Irish moors, but it's constrained. "Your experiences as a boy chained it up and then you saw in Vietnam what happens when people let the beast loose, and you knew how dangerous your beast was so you added another padlock on it."

Consistent with Buddhist practice, I have tried through meditation to calmly release my storehouse of anger and resentments through a deep examination of their roots. Buddhism centers on understanding the context of suffering in the world, both our own and the suffering of others, and on release from delusion and suffering through meditation and insight into the true nature of reality.

Bradshaw includes in his book a checklist of thirty-six personality traits that are indicators of "adult children of dysfunctional families." When I highlighted those traits that applied to me to a significant degree either currently or at any time of my adult life, the list jumped off the page with fluorescent yellow. One trait that particularly struck me was labeled "internalized shame," with this description: "You feel flawed as a human being. You ... hide behind a role or an addiction or character trait like ... blame, criticism, [or] perfectionism."

Nailed me. The book helped me understand how my character defects were strategies I used to transfer my shame to others. My perfectionism, for example, was a great way to not feel shame. How could I be vulnerable if I never made a mistake? And, since I felt exceptional—a pompous ass, some might say— I could maintain my moral superiority, at least in my immature mind.

Bradshaw advises letting go the notion of placing a positive or negative value on the emotion of shame and instead encourages us to embrace it so that it can be restored as a feeling and not a state of being. "Healthy shame," he writes, "tells us we are finite, limited and prone to mistakes .... I can feel shame over some things I've done without concluding I'm defective as a person." Later in his book he adds, "Shame as an emotion moves me to do something about what I've done. Shame triggers my guilt, which triggers my conscience. I can then take action to repair the damage that I had done. With guilt I made a *mistake* and I can correct it whenever possible .... Healthy shame literally means modesty, awe and reverence."

The following diagram illustrates my therapy. I worked harder than at any time in my life to understand at a fundamental level the inter-linking of the combat events that caused the PTSD with the childhood trauma that preceded them in my case. Only until I could bring full compassion as regards the effects these past traumas had on me did I have the emotional maturity to forgive myself and others. Therapy has helped me with the lifelong process of integrating all of these experiences as being part of who I fully am, and to learn and grow from them.

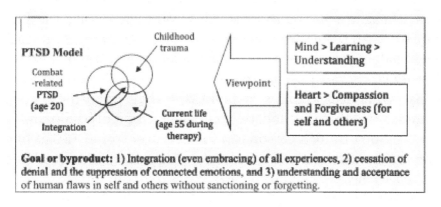

Embracing The Ghosts And Accepting The Love And Help From Others—The Fourth Tool

After nine intensive months with Thomas and Cynthia serving as witnesses to my trauma stories, I knew I had gone about as far as I could go with therapy. My heart work had given full voice to the "tender-hearted boy" and my headwork had integrated it with the strong side of my personality. My new appreciation of the power parents wield over their powerless and impression-able children led to a balanced story about my upbringing that incorporated *both* its positive and negative aspects. The same be-came true for my Vietnam story. I could objectively identify my emotions and give them a balanced voice without letting them overwhelm me in the process. I learned to recognize the fine line between repressing feelings and honoring them by fully ac-knowledging the consequences of my losses and trauma. While I'm much more emotional now and I still can be flooded with those same deep feelings of sadness, I understand them now. Thomas said that this holistic approach is a sign of healing.

I don't think a person can fully recover from PTSD as one can from a cold or a broken leg. As a wise person said, trauma is always with you, but you can learn to carry it differently.

Our large picture window offers a broad view of falling snow blanketing our front yard and the city street in a silent, seemingly pristine world. "I'm done," I announce to Cynthia. "Thomas agrees. He predicted I'd know when the time came to stop therapy." For the fortieth time, she sits opposite me—her impossibly curly hair haloed in the brilliant backlight from the picture window—as I re-late the minutia of my last fifty-minute session and take notes. The reporting takes longer than the session did, and her "ahhs" and occasional questions and comments punctuate my monologue and affirm her attention is unwavering.

"Are you sure you're done?" she asks. I am. I put down my notes, join her on the couch, and wrap her in my arms. She wraps me in non-judgment, understanding, and unconditional love. A spoken thank you can never suffice. I owe this wise woman my life. I am hers for the rest of mine. The snow cannot muffle our tears of joy.

PART V

A Collection of Essays

10. THE ARC
OF A LEAP

Mindful observation is the element which nourishes the tree of understanding, and compassion and love are the most beautiful flowers .... If love is in our heart, every thought, word, and deed can bring about a miracle.
　　　　　　　　　　—Thich Nhat Hanh, *Peace is Every Step*

Sometimes life progresses from one stepping-stone to another. Logical. Incremental. Predictable. Sometimes it requires a leap, and the arc of a leap depends on firm footing at the launch rather than a safe landing place. In mid-July, 1968, I was as sure-footed as a Floridian on a frozen Ohio lake when I received a call from my Borromeo High School Seminary buddy with an invite for a trip to New York City with three other former classmates. I leapt at the chance and the arc changed my life.

In the two years between the time of his call and our high school graduation, I had only seen Henry a couple of times. Second year college captured most of our attention; he a business student at John Carroll University; I an architecture student at Kent State University.

"I've got some time off between my summer classes and when I have to go back to work at Republic Steel, so the timing's perfect!" I could feel excitement in Henry's voice. Normally, he delivered his words with objective precision as if he were accounting for their use from a stockroom in the back of his mind. "Jerry, Ken, and Brian are driving there and they already booked a room in Manhattan. I thought we could hitch it in and save money," he added, "that is, unless you can score a car." I told Henry I could barely afford food after paying for gas for my little Honda motorcycle, tuition, and rent for my tiny off-campus hovel. My sporadic summer jobs as a carpenter's assistant in Kent kept me a pauper in terms of cash but rich in free time.

"Great," Henry concluded. "I'll find us a room."

With a plan in place, the leap began. On Thursday morning, July 24, I hitched the sixty miles to Henry's campus in Cleveland's University Heights neighborhood and spent the night in an empty bed in his dormitory. Next morning, out went our thumbs in the direction of our future.

After several rides between long waits on the on-ramps of the Ohio and Pennsylvania turnpikes, a small straight-bodied truck pulled over as the sun was beginning to set behind us about midway through Pennsylvania. It was an old International; so decrepit it might have come from the set of the Depression-era movie, *The Grapes of Wrath*. I hopped up on the foothold and peered in through the open passenger window. Instead of Henry Fonda, I saw a face as black as the interior the ancient truck.

"Where to?" came the gruff question from the driver.

Henry was a step behind me and we both simultaneously intoned, "New York City," as if we were still singing in the bass section of our high school choir.

"Get in. That's where I'm going," he said over the throaty rumble of the engine.

There was a single passenger seat, grease stained with a long diagonal rip down its center. I propped our two small backpacks as a backrest atop the trucker detritus in the back of the cab and parked my one-sixty-pound frame on the black engine cowling that squatted between the two seats. A stale cigar smoldered in an ashtray that was probably last emptied after the war —the First World War. Henry hopped up into the passenger seat with the same grace he displayed on the basketball court as one of the star players in our class. Immediately, our driver—I don't remember his name—dropped into low range with a horrible grinding of tortured gears and then clutched it into first. We jerked forward through eight gearshifts and eventually topped out at fifty-five heading east on the Pennsylvania Turnpike toward the greatest city in the world.

Even with the windows wide open for the cooler evening air, the cab was a foul-smelling oven and my engine cowling seat was the main burner. I slipped a well-thumbed girlie magazine underneath me for some protection. Butt to butt. Soon, the heat and the reverberating drone from the truck engine lulled us both to sleep with "MacArthur Park" playing on the tinny AM radio as counterpoint.

Borromeo High School Seminary was the birthplace of Henry's and my friendship and the cradle for my mental and spiritual awakening. As the Buddhist saying goes, when the student is ready, the teacher will arrive. I was very ready when I entered the seminary in 1962 and my teachers were waiting for me. I soon came to respect their dedication and knowledge, their humility and authentic spirituality. To say these priests were very good teachers is like saying Mozart was very good at putting little dots and lines on paper. I wanted to be like these wise, holy priests; these Christ figures. They were my rock stars, as confident in their celibate skins and black cassocks as Mick Jagger was with his guitar and skin-tight jeans. Instead of singing "I can't get no satisfaction," they taught the ideal of "offering it up to Jesus;" all of it—the difficult and painful as well as the fun and enriching. My teachers stressed integration of the body, mind, and spirit aspects of life. They were in the world but not of the world.

As a thirteen-year-old entering the seminary, I arrived with my childish understanding of Catholic mysticism—I had swallowed the dogma whole—and my teachers helped me transform it into an ethical framework upon which I built my life. But I had a vocation to become a seminarian, not to become a priest; a vocation to search, not to swallow whole without chewing. Although my ties to the Church eventually frayed (I left the faith two years after our New York trip), I have always treasured this four-year experience and its primary life lesson. I still strive to live in the present moment as my current Buddhist teachers suggest.

"Hey! Wake up! We're here! New York City."

I tried to shake some overcooked neurons awake and reconnect the seared synapses of my brain. *New York City ... New York City. NEW YORK CITY!! We're here*, I thought. *Wait, where are the bright lights and skyscrapers?* In the sallow illumination of the streetlights were tired, multi-storied apartments that lined both sides of the dismally dark street. The truck had returned to the set of that Henry Fonda movie.

"Where are we?" Henry asked.

"New York City," our driver repeated, now a little agitated. "Harlem, actually. You boys know Harlem don't you?"

The whole world knew Harlem. The '64 Harlem riot was the harbinger of the decade's later black civil rights uprisings that rocked Watts, Detroit, and—the year before our trip—the Hough neighborhood in Cleveland.

"Hell, don't you sweat a thing, boys. See that traffic light up ahead? That's 125th. Take a left there and walk a half-mile or so west to Amsterdam, then take another left and go south 'til you hit Broadway. Ya can't miss it." He was right. It was about three in the morning and otherwise dangerous Harlem let us two naive white boys walk peacefully through the neighborhood until we reached the lights of Broadway and the hotel Henry had found for us three miles south in Midtown Manhattan.

Had Henry the power of the Internet in 1968, he could have read this glowing reference to his hotel choice in *King's Handbook of New York City*: "The Broadway Central at 667 to 675 Broadway ... is one of the largest (if not the largest) in New York, having 640 sleeping-rooms, with comfortable accommodations for over 1,000 guests. It is a solid and spacious structure ... . When the present hotel was built, it was one of the finest hotel structures on the continent." Problem was, this was written in 1892 when the hotel was already a quarter-century old. Conditions had changed a bit over the next three-quarters of a century before we arrived. Like the truck that had brought us to this city, the Broadway Central was long overdue for the scrap heap. The lobby, with its mirrors and worn, red carpet was small and dismal; the kind you'd pick if you were a locations scout for a movie with a scene that featured prostitutes and rooms rented by the hour. I remember walking up a lot of stairs because the elevator, one of the earliest the Otis Company built (it originally ran on steam), was either closed for repairs or should have been. Stairs are supposed to stay in place, but the ones Henry and I climbed were broken and pieces had actually fallen away. We had to hug the walls on the way up—and I wondered what lived in those walls.

Five years after Henry and I collapsed on hammock-like mattresses in a room that still carried the subtle perfume of stale cigars, the Broadway Central Hotel collapsed into the center of Broadway. A 1973 newspaper article reported that a crooked architect had filed bogus plans with the New York City Inspections Department to modify a basement wall, omitting the fact that it was a load-bearing structure. The story holds special importance for me now as a city planner. But that night in 1968, a couple hours from sunrise, Henry and I were far too tired to register interest in anything other than sleep.

Too few hours later, Henry and I walked the half-mile to the twenty-seven story Lexington Hotel at 48th and Lexington to see our other high school classmates, Jerry, Ken, and Brian, who had driven Brian's '67 Pontiac Le Mans into the city a day earlier. I was struck by the contrast of our respective hotel lobbies. Theirs had a mirror-like marble floor, elegant chandeliers, and guests who did not appear to have slept in their clothes. For this article, I checked to see if theirs had also collapsed in the meantime and discovered that this elegant, old beauty was now thriving with the Radisson chain. In fact, they are offering a wonderful "Summer Special" that not only includes accommodations for one person, but also a "Summer Surprise gift bag containing two high quality New York postcards, an 'I Love NY' mug, a metallic New York keychain, and an artistic Radisson Lexington tee." Hard to top that for a mere $239 a night.

Before the concierge could throw us out as vagrants, Henry found the lobby phone. Brian answered and said they would meet us in the lobby because they were on their way to a basement room full of mysterious lights that promised a golden tan in minutes. Henry and I tagged along having no clue what he was talking about. We found a room just large enough for the five of us to stand, with four-foot florescent-like tubes mounted vertically on two walls. Someone found a switch and the walls buzzed to life with an intense flood of light. We peeled off all of our clothes and giggled a little at the novelty of it all. I recall a little bell going off periodically and figured it meant to rotate for a nice even tan. After several bell tones and rotations, we decided we'd had enough even though the twenty minutes we'd spent there had no apparent effect on our skin tone. We weren't even very warm.

I don't recall what we did the rest of the morning and early afternoon, but I vividly remember how, by late afternoon, our skins, scorched from head to mid-thigh—no exceptions—began their screams of pain. I filled the tub in their hotel room with cool water and I swear I heard sizzles as I slid slowly in until only my nose was above the water. Then I drifted off to sleep.

By early evening, we decided to sightsee and get some food, despite our tenderized exteriors and the still hot city streets. Only Jerry and I, who were burned the worst, were still hurting. The five of us took turns leading the way along a zigzag route through the canyons of this imposing and seemingly dangerous city, moving with the single-minded maneuvers of a school of small fish that finds security in numbers. For all but Ken, it was our first time in New York City and she was a feast for our impressionable eyes. She presented her best and her worst, often within the same block. Skyscraper cathedrals ablaze with lights drew our eyes heavenward, while bedraggled men, babbling mindlessly amid overtopped cans of composting garbage on the crowded sidewalks, grounded us in the realities of big city life. To this day, a whiff from the hot entrails of a passing garbage truck still taps directly into a cellular memory of those New York City smells as if the fetid aroma of slow-cooked sidewalk garbage had seeped into me like primordial ooze. I recall stepping around the homeless sleeping in doorways and avoiding a disheveled man with a two-foot-high stack of hats on his head—all kinds of hats. Maybe they made him feel less intimidated by the buildings. Woody Guthrie's line, "It's a rich man's world," came to mind.

As evening approached, the grandest site of them all was before us at 5th Avenue and 34th St.: the Eighth Wonder of the World and the city's quintessential landmark, the Empire State Building. Like every American tourist before us since the movie's release in 1933, we pictured a fifty-foot ape climbing the sleek limestone and stainless-steel walls all the way up to the dirigible mooring mast at its peak. Standing in a long line for the elevator ride, my excitement built as if it were for Ohio's Geauga Lake's roller coaster, the Clipper. Finally, the gleaming brass Art Deco elevator doors closed around us and soon the pain from my swelling inner ears was added to the sting from my sunburn.

"Swallow. Swallow hard," the smartly uniformed doorman ordered. He was used to rubes unaware of the effects of the 1,250-foot climb to the Observation Deck at the 102nd floor. After two elevator rides to the top, the doors slowly opened onto the place where my world was about to change. No, not architectural splendor. We spied girls, three of them. Good-looking girls that looked our age. *Wow!*

We experienced the same fear-triggered instinctual dilemma of fight or flight and its modern manifestations, pursue or sightsee. Since Brian, Ken, and Jerry were still in the seminary, one step toward these three beautiful young women put in jeopardy their vocation to the celibate priesthood. Hyperbole? Hardly. Years of rigid discipline toward the dream of becoming a priest builds a fortress of determination; a mighty dam intended to hold back the torrential rivers of testosterone that race through every young man. My memory of this dilemma as a high school seminarian is not only vivid, it's visceral. I remember praying hard for a wet dream to relieve some of the explosive pressure. Then, my sexuality was the enemy of my chastity. Later, it became the hinge that swung open a door to a new view of the world. My three seminarian friends, on summer break outside their semi-cloistered walls, must have been experiencing hormones on hair-trigger alert when we spotted the three girls up ahead.

Oh my God! They're looking our way—and smiling!

There is a third survival option—freeze, and while my former classmates did just that, I pursued the first option. Having left the seminary after our high school graduation, I was no longer bound by the Medieval Church's policy decision in 1139 to prohibit priests from marrying because Rome worried that clerics' children might inherit Church property and create dynasties. I had my own hormonal rapids flowing and I figured flight and freeze were no longer moral necessities.

After I went over and started talking with the three girls, the rest of my classmates joined in. With the forgiving awkwardness inherent in youthful inexperience, we took turns introducing ourselves and wove in the basics of our seminary and college involvements and our work. They had just come from dinner at Momma Leone's at 44th and 7th Avenue. We learned that Jane, a tall thin girl with long brown hair that cascaded in waves to her shoulders, was a year older than we seminarians. She had dropped out of her studies at the University of Minnesota after two years to work full time in reservations with Northwest Airlines at the Minneapolis-Saint Paul International Airport. Her sister, Judy, only eighteen years old, was a shorter version of Jane and had just graduated high school. Recently, she told me she found the entire New York experience to be "a little overwhelming."

But the one who caught my eye was the striking blonde with the asymmetrical hairstyle. Cynthia was the tallest of the three and the shapeliest. There was something about her face. When she smiled, her entire face joined in with a fluid transformation that spoke of authenticity and a lot of practice. Like Jane, she had graduated a year earlier than we boys. She was completing her general requirements at the U of M while working full time as a legal secretary for an old and prestigious law firm in St. Paul. Right away, I noticed her air of easy self-confidence that came from refusing to take any guff from pretentious, high-powered attorneys.

We easily fell in together and became a group. As we walked around the circumference of the Observation Deck and took in the incredible cityscape from this most idyllic of vantage points, we began to pair up. "Brian was real cute," Jane told me recently, "and Judy thought so too." Soon, Jane and Brian were settled in side-by-side and engaged in a two-party conversation. Like pheromones on the wind, natural forces beyond our understanding subtly drew Cynthia and me toward each other. A spark arced between us, triggered a heart flutter, and fused a connection however small; a psychic synapse.

We decided to walk the mile and a half straight down Fifth Avenue to Washington Square in Greenwich Village—the hippest place on the planet. Once there, a couple of us struck up a conversation with some members of the popular folk singing group, Up With People. They suggested we take in the singer in a nearby club. A small neon sign steered us down sidewalk stairs to a basement bar where we heard a performer sing and play his guitar. His raspy style had one leg in the Bohemian/Beatnik era of the '50s and the other in the folk era of the '60s. One of the draws of New York was the state's drinking age of eighteen, which was three years earlier than most other states, including Ohio and Minnesota. The performer added to the mystique of sharing a beer with groovy chicks in a basement bar in the Village. Like most mystiques, they're as short-lived as the attention span of the young, so we decided to take the subway to Coney Island ten miles away. Jane had had enough mystique for the day so she took a cab back to the Taft Hotel where the three of them were staying while the rest of us navigated the subway to the Island.

We hung out for a time in the carnival portion of the venerable amusement park and Ken won a pink ceramic pig by pitching softballs at clay milk bottles. Recently, he told me how much he enjoyed the crash that pig made in the alley when he dropped it out the Lexington's twentieth floor hotel window the next day. When the rest of the group decided to call it a night, Cynthia and I said we would go for a walk on the beach.

Each step down the beach took us further from the crowds, lights, and noise, and deeper into the night and its invitation for intimacy. We talked. We opened up to each other in a way I had never before experienced; a mutual mind-meld. We compared family history, shared our values and beliefs, and laughed over our most embarrassing moments. She had a sense of humor that doubled me over with delight. I told her how I loved my four years in the seminary and all about my newfound passion for architecture. The physical mimicked the verbal and, in incremental stages, we fell in step with each other. Then, when the natural swing of our arms brought our hands close, I slipped mine around hers not daring to look at her at the same time. Walking hand-in-hand felt like an old habit rather than our first touch. We sat for a long time on the dark and isolated beach and sang a few lines to each other from We Five's "You Were On My Mind." The soft rhythmic surge of the waves filled in long gaps of comfortable silence.

Like the turbulence of the crashing waves, the conflicts of our era tumbled around our talk about the future. I told her I had enlisted in the Marines and expected to go to Vietnam and she told me about her anti-war protests. America was embroiled in its most contentious time since the Civil War. Within families all across the land, civil wars were raging between kids entranced by the profound changes sweeping the social landscape and their parents who tenaciously hung on to the values that had served them through the Great Depression and World War Two. The sex-drugs-and-rock-and-roll generals—Dr. Alfred

Kinsey, Dr. Timothy Leary, and the Beatles, faced the God-and-country generals—Bishop Fulton J. Sheen, Richard M. Nixon, and actual General William Westmoreland. Our parents' views seemed obsolete, anachronistic. We dismissed them as dinosaurs that couldn't see the meteorite coming.

We were kids in Dodge-Em cars having the chaotic ride of our lives but always wondering who's going to blindside us. Between 1965 and 1968, assassins removed our leaders Malcolm X, Dr. Martin Luther King, Che Guevara, and—a month before our New York City trip, Bobby Kennedy. The same year of our trip, North Vietnamese and Viet Cong troops launched their most devastating push of the war, the 1968 Tet Offensive, and laid siege to Khe Sanh in the bloodiest battle of the war for U.S. soldiers. U.S. troop levels exceeded half a million, U.S. deaths passed the thirty thousand mark, and fifty thousand antiwar protesters marched on the Pentagon.

Vietnam set parent against child, brother against sister, lover against lover, and past values of "peace through strength" against a nascent value system based on peace through love. Cynthia couldn't understand the half-baked reasons I offered for my enlistment (it took the writing of a book thirty years later for me to understand them), and I was jealous that the draft exempted her gender.

As we walked off our lovely beach and boarded the subway to head back to Manhattan, our mind-meld continued. We didn't want to disconnect, so we rode the rails for hours. Finally, sometime in the middle of that timeless night, we left the trains and I walked her up 7th Ave. to the Taft at 50th St.

We kissed goodnight.

Every sappy romantic movie tries to depict that moment when you part after that first kiss and then have a few seconds for the electricity to spark from your lips and then surge throughout your entire nervous system. It links to the day Santa came through and gave you the Lionel train that you had prayed for to him, to Jesus, and to St. Jude, the Saint for Impossible Causes. I was drifting somewhere in Einstein's space-time continuum without a compass, so I just kept repeating her name over and over as I walked away. I sang out, "Cyn-thee-a, Cyn-thee-a, I've just met a girl named Cyn-thee-a," to any of the Jets or Sharks who might be listening.

Cynthia felt it too. She returned to the Taft and woke up Jane to tell her, "I met the man I could marry."

I was too buzzed that night to head back to sleep with whatever lived in the walls of the Broadway Central a mile north, so I walked aimlessly around Midtown for a time. I passed a secluded grotto on the grounds of St. Patrick's Cathedral and noticed a covered walkway that connected a small building to the great church. It offered a low flat roof that seemed an inviting place to contemplate the meaning of the remarkable chain of events so I climbed up. Propped against St. Pat's warm stone wall and hidden by shadows, I drifted off to sleep. An hour or so later, I climbed down to finish my trip to my hotel when I heard voices. In the middle of the night in the middle of a city of eight million, these voices were familiar. Across the street and coming towards me were Brian and Ken on either side of Jerry. I called out and ran over to tell them all about my incredibly wonderful evening but they immediately explained that Jerry had gone blind. When the pain had gotten so bad, they found a doctor in a nearby clinic who gave him a prescription and directions to an all-night pharmacy.

"It was those lights," Brian explained. "Jerry didn't close his eyes and they fried his retinas."

Jerry hadn't said a word but I could read the pain from the grimace on his face. I joined them and we found the store. While Brian and Ken went in to buy the medicine, I stayed with Jerry outside on a bench that was shaded from the glare of the florescent and neon. Either Jerry's eyes were oozing something or he was silently crying; I couldn't tell.

While we waited, two prostitutes approached us. I had never seen anyone like them. They had more curves than Yankee pitcher, Whitey Ford, and clothes that clung so tightly I thought it was just their way of saying thank you for the opportunity.

The big hair, flashy jewelry, and heavy makeup said more about price than the hood ornament on a Cadillac. One was black and the other white and both were large. Very large! Towering well over six feet each in their spiked heels, they were pumped-up proportionately and as overpowering as the city itself. I stammered through a lame explanation of having to take care of my injured friend and they left chuckling to each other in voices much deeper than I expected.

Jerry felt better the next day. To keep the magic alive, we gave a call over to the Taft to see what our new friends were doing. They were interested in the Guggenheim but needed to get back in time to see the Broadway hit, "Hello Dolly," a version that featured Pearl Bailey and the Cab Calloway Orchestra. At the Guggenheim, I devoted more attention to impressing Cynthia with my knowledge of Frank Lloyd Wright's masterpiece than appreciating the art within it.

On Sunday, the girls' vacation was over and I rode the train with them to JFK International. They were flying Northwest Airlines and Jane was flying stand-by as an airline employee. Cynthia donated her regular fare seat to her so that we could spend a couple more hours together. We had a tender parting with tears. I waved at the departing plane as if Cynthia could see me through the thick plastic windows; and she waved back at me as if the crisp morning sun weren't blinding me. Later that afternoon, Henry and I boarded a Greyhound and headed back to Cleveland. During our twelve-hour return trip, I thought back over every aspect of the extraordinary encounter.

A month and a half after that New York City trip, I reported to Paris Island, South Carolina for Marine Corps boot camp while Cynthia returned home to continue her anti-war efforts. Over the next five years, we came together on four more occasions that totaled about twenty days. We lived through Vietnam and its aftermath, our respective failed marriages and divorces, the birth of her Jessica, and the loss of our innocence. At the end of this five-year arc, I finally found a safe landing place— in her arms. On July 21, 1973, I married this wonderful woman and eighteen-month-old Jessica and began a habit of making our leaps together, now hand-in-hand.

Many years ago, I took a chance. I took a leap and I met someone. We planted a seed that sprouted and grew.

11. THE PASSION
OF A HUMANIST

Men rarely, if ever, managed to dream up a god superior to them-
selves. Most gods have the manners and morals of a spoiled child.
—Robert A. Heinlein, science-fiction author

With or without religion, you would have good people doing good
things and evil people doing evil things. But for good people to do evil
things, that takes religion.
—Mark Twain

G rowing up in a strict Catholic household, I knew that the
Passion story was the central message of Christianity
but I still had a difficult time with it. My childhood stories included Jolly St. Nick who brought me wonderful presents,
the cuddly Easter Bunny who brought me candy, and the generous Tooth Fairy who paid me a shiny quarter for every tooth
I tearfully lost. Then came the story of my savior, Jesus, whose
grisly death by torture overshadowed the softer tales of his wise
and peaceful spirit. By six, I had outgrown all but the Jesus story.

It took me fifteen more years and a war before I finally
abandoned my childhood faith in that story too. How could I
trust my religion to guide me as I faced life's challenges in a time
of pervasive violence when its central theme was an ancient
story about a divine parent who demanded the violent death

of his child in order to "take away the sins of the world?" This notion of a narcissistic, filicidal god only makes sense as a very human creation for tribal/societal control. Successful religions advance the thinking of the day with a useful message. If they don't evolve with advancing human thought, their original usefulness appears petrified centuries later.

Rabbi Abraham Joshua Heschel, in his book, *God in Search of Man: A Philosophy of Judaism*, wrote about this: "It is customary to blame secular science and anti-religious philosophy for the eclipse of religion in modern society. It would be more honest to blame religion for its own defeats. Religion declined not because it was refuted, but because it became irrelevant, dull, oppressive, insipid. When faith is completely replaced by creed, worship by discipline, love by habit, when the crisis of today is ignored because of the splendor of the past, when faith becomes an heirloom rather than a living fountain, when religion speaks only in the name of authority rather than with the voice of compassion, its message becomes meaningless."

Now, so many years later, I can look back at the toxic messages I received from the Roman Catholic Church. I know other people find different, more redeeming messages in Christianity, but these were the ones I heard in my childhood, lined up as the rings marking a target:

The innermost ring dealt with the denigration of self. My parents and my church taught me that only Jesus' life was meaningful in and of itself. The toxic message was that it was only through his life, and primarily his suffering, that we had any individual intrinsic value, provided, of course, we were Catholics in the state of grace. All self-worth came through Jesus' suffering and redemption.

With this principle, the Church created its first tool for its power grab. The Passion story's focus on Jesus' blind obedience to a self-serving god sanctioned suffering and silence in the face of abuse. The corollary message I got as a kid was that nothing I could accomplish could compare with what Jesus gave up to take on his human character, and nothing I could ever suffer could compare with his crucifixion.

The second concentric ring, moving out, is the exclusivity clause common to Christianity and Islam. This toxic message declared that we believers had the one true faith. We deserved eternal happiness after death while nonbelievers deserved eternal damnation. Our sacred mission was to convert the nonbelievers and, if we failed, to persecute them or die as martyrs trying. Of course, this message was too raw for most people, so the Church sugarcoated it with the stories of missionaries and its charitable works. This exclusivity clause led to a false sense of moral superiority that has fueled much of the hatred, prejudice, and conflict in the world since the rise of these two monotheistic religions. In his lengthy and authoritative book, *Constantine's Sword*, James Carroll extensively describes the Catholic Church's long history of institutionalized persecution of the "other:" namely, Jews, Muslims, and those it defined as heretics (a word derived from the Greek meaning "able to choose").

Once freed of this of construct, I became open to the positive and negative aspects of other religions.

In the third ring, the toxic message was about sex and gender. The priests and nuns taught me that all sexuality, outside of that needed for procreation between a man and a woman married in the Roman Catholic Church, was base and evil. I was so thoroughly inculcated by age thirteen, I thought I had a vocation to the priesthood. After four years in Borromeo Seminary, something began to stir in me, especially near the end of my senior year in high school. At Mass one morning, I realized that while Jesus may have given me the gift of a vocation, he neglected to include the gift of celibacy. Due to the Church's medieval policy requiring a celibate, male-only clergy, you cannot have one without the other, so I left two weeks later. I wanted a family and I was tired of praying for wet dreams.

Later, I realized that most of the Church's socio-political positions stem from ancient dogmatic assumptions regarding gender and sexuality. I also recalled how the messages from my grade school nuns about femininity were limited to stories about the Virgin Mary, a woman the Church uniquely elevated for having fulfilled her primary role as a mother without the taint of intercourse; and about "Holy Mother the Church," a misnomer for an organization run exclusively by and primarily for men.

In the fourth and outermost ring, the toxic message is supernatural. I learned that the true purpose of this life was as a test to determine the appropriate afterlife. Life was just the all-nighter before the final exam. Christianity, of course, is not the first or only religion that assumes a gatekeeper role for the Heaven and Hell that religion invented to capture and retain power. I recall a fantasy of Heaven as a child as a place where I could eat Milky Way candy bars forever. I have not heard a more mature description since. I share the view of Karen Armstrong, a writer and former Catholic nun, "Religion is supposed to be about losing your ego, not preserving it eternally in optimum conditions."

The Church's monopoly on the supernatural also incorporated the dualism central to Western religion; the notion of separating the "good" and "evil" aspects of human nature and anthropomorphizing them into supernatural entities called God and the Devil. The notion trapped me in a juvenile's world where I responded to the rewards and punishments meted out by my parents. This coercive message helps us shirk adult accountability in this life. We joke that, "the Devil made me do it," or that our accomplishment was only possible through Jesus' help. As I learned in Vietnam, we humans don't need a devil to do horrific things, and we don't need a god to be heroic. Everyone is capable of both given the right circumstances.

Unlike some religions that offer a smorgasbord choice of dogmas according to taste, my Church said take it one hundred percent or take a hike. My first explorations of sex and love as a teenager and the lessons of Vietnam spawned doubt, and that doubt led quickly to the complete collapse of my Catholic house of dogma cards and the start of my spiritual hike. I could no longer accept the notion of an anthropomorphized god that changed its mind based on a heartfelt prayer from one of its creatures. I had not yet learned that the beneficiary of prayer and its secular equivalent, meditation, is the devotee, not the deity.

I recall Christmas Eve night in 1969 in the midst of a lull in the fighting. Battle-hardened, with three quarters of my tour of duty behind me, I was tired and as cynical as acid. I recall how the faint sound of carols drew me to the squat sandbagged building that served as a chapel on our fire support base. I stood in the doorway and listened in the glow of candlelight to the heartfelt a cappella singing of "Silent Night." Embodied in that soft refrain was all the allure of my youthful idealism, the familiar comfort of my religion, the energizing tingle that emanated from my worship, and the lifesaving hope of eternal deliverance and salvation. I paused a moment to take it all in, then I joined in the singing from that doorway. I reached out for this lifeline, desperately hoping that doing so could make sense out of my experience. Before the song was over, reality dropped a heavy hand on my shoulder and reminded me that I never sensed God was with me in my foxhole. I wiped away the embarrassment of tears and went back to my hooch to clean my rifle. It was my last day as a Christian but just another day in Vietnam.

There's another side, of course. Integrated with the toxic aspects of the Church's teachings were ideas that shaped my core commitment. Since a child, I adopted a belief that my happiness depended on service on behalf of ideas and people I believed in, and playing a role in something larger than myself. That imprinting steered me at thirteen to the seminary in service to my Church, at nineteen to the military in service to "God and country," and at twenty-five to a public service career. It still directs me in my work and in other aspects of my life. The faith of my childhood served as training wheels for my freewheeling exploration of deeper meanings as I matured spiritually.

Vietnam was the place where my core commitment crashed into reality. Vietnam was the place where chaplains blessed my fellow Marines and me in the name of our God before we went into free fire zones on search and destroy missions to kill the godless Communists and anything else that moved. War —that atrocity-producing machine—forced me to confront the lies my church and country used to accomplish their ends.

The betrayal is the hardest part. The pain of betrayal equals the weight of the investments of love, trust, belief, time, conviction, and concern. I was a believer but I came to see the perversity of my Church asking me to sacrifice this life in the name of an afterlife, and my country asking me to sacrifice a peasant's life in the name of the American Empire. To return to the Passion story, it's about another betrayal; a betrayal by a father of his son. We make our gods in our own image. How much pain and suffering could we avoid if only parents stood up to their gods and countries and said, "No, you will not take my child to appease your ego!" Jesus' father-god lacked that kind of courage.

Many Christians see the scale of Christ's suffering as evidence of his love for humankind. I wonder if they would also accept its logical antithesis: Had Jesus not suffered so terribly—say he happened to live the normal life of a rabbi with a wife, kids, and a decent living, would his followers then have to believe he loved them less? Since many modern biblical scholars conclude that very little of the Jesus story can be supported, much less confirmed, via standard anthropological methods and other contemporary sources, some hold this and other versions of Jesus' life as more likely than the heavily edited and mythologized version in the Church's Canonical Gospels. Like the Arthurian Legend, scholars can't sort the myth from the slim historical evidence; they can't separate the fiction from the cruci-fiction. [23]

The Passion story was an ugly movie that the Church of my childhood projected relentlessly in my head until, as an adult, I finally had the guts to pull the plug and fire the projectionist. For many years now, I've embraced my doubt as an agnostic and studied Buddhism. I now watch a new movie in my head and I like it. It's about humans redeeming themselves and each other in this life in synch with the rest of the universe. It's about love, not violence and I call it *The Passion of a Humanist.*

Fundamental to the rift with my father was his inability or unwillingness to examine ethics, religion, philosophy, or spirituality through any lens other than his orthodox version of Catholicism. He believed that to qualify as a religion, it had to have a creed of religious beliefs that its members were required to accept (as does the IRS under Section 501(c)(3) of the U.S. Tax Code). When I explained that Cynthia and I were long-time active members of our local Unitarian Universalist church and that the religion has no prescribed creed, he asked, what's the point if you don't have to believe in something, at least God? He could not separate agnosticism's absence of belief in anything supernatural from atheism's belief that there is no God. When I tried to describe my interest in Buddhism and explained that, at its most basic level, it's a creedless philosophy of living and not a religion, he repeated his question.

I recall trying to explain to Dad how Ken Wilber delineates the two differing types of religion in his book *Grace and Grit.* Wilber, who is a scholar of religion and philosophy and the author of over twenty books, says that virtually all the great religions of the world recognize the difference between "exoteric" or *outer* religion, and "esoteric" or *inner* religion. This is what he wrote:

> Exoteric or "outer" religion is mythic religion, religion that is terribly concrete and literal, that really believes, for example, that Moses parted the Red Sea, that Christ was born from a virgin, that the world was created in six days, that manna once literally rained down from Heaven, and so on. … If you believe all the myths, you are saved; if not, you go to Hell—no discussion. Now you find that type of religion the world over—fundamentalism … .

> Esoteric, or inner religion tends to be more contemplative and mystical and experiential, and less cognitive and conceptual. Esoteric religion asks you to believe

nothing on faith or obediently swallow any dogma. Rather, esoteric religion is a set of personal experiments that you conduct scientifically in the laboratory of your own awareness. Like all good science, it is based on direct experience, no mere belief or wish, and it is publicly checked or validated by a peer group of those who have also performed the experiment. The experiment is meditation.[24]

I told Dad that I had been in search of the esoteric since I stopped believing in the exoteric aspects of Christianity back when I was twenty. He repeated his question and I could only shake my head and walk away. I was as unsuccessful with proselytizing my beliefs with him as he was with me.

An excerpted version of this story was published in *Cairns, the Unity Church Journal of the Arts*, Vol. 1, No. 1, fall 2009, Unity Church Unitarian, St. Paul, MN.

12. GROWING UP WITH J.B.

T hese pages include so much about the troubles I had with my father. To offer a counterbalance, I'm including a few short stories I wrote about him. I read the second and third at his eightieth birthday party in 1997. He told me he really enjoyed it. I wrote the last two to share with my siblings.

The Handshake

Lunch With Soupy Sales was a favorite children's TV show when I was perhaps five or six. One Saturday morning, probably in the early-1950s, my father told me to get in the car. He had a surprise—just for me. The two of us drove to the Burke Lakefront Airport in downtown Cleveland and joined a small gathering of kids and their parents in the parking lot. It wasn't until I saw the *real* Soupy Sales walking towards the crowd that I realized how special was this gift.

The crowd surrounded Sales but I could see nothing but other kids and adult butts—that is, until I felt my dad lift me up, plow his way to within a few feet of this child celebrity, and extend me over the shoulder of the man in front of us.

"Stick your hand out!" Dad said over the din from excited kids. I did and Soupy Sales shook it. Electricity shot through me, the excitement of touching greatness. Meeting the Pope, Jesus Christ, or even a player on the Cleveland Indians team would not have matched that thrill.

Thanks Dad.

The Not-So-Great Train Wreck

My dad is about to celebrate his 80th birthday. He has suffered heart attacks, congestive heart failure, and the shutdown of every major organ in his body save his brain. He has weathered the death of his wife of forty-nine years, one of his sons, and every other member of his immediate family. He survived the Great Depression, World War Two, and Cleveland winters. Not to discount the difficulty the above list represents, still, his greatest achievement is probably surviving me. Don't get me wrong, I'm not trying to puff up my own self-importance. I just think if offered a Faustian Bargain for a son that fit the mold he had in mind, instead of me, he would have paid a very high price. Even something like, say, another tour of duty on Guam, or another decade of seven-days-a-week work, or not seeing the Tribe win the Series in 1948.

Of course, it wasn't just my doing. I had a lot of help from my brothers and sisters. It was probably the mountain of challenges we built together for Dad to overcome that honed his coping skills so he could surmount all the other barriers life placed before him. The following story about an early Christmas morning in 1955 recounts just one of those challenges.

It was still dark when I awoke with the vision that this was going to be the greatest of all Christmases. I shook my little brother, Denny, from his twin bed on the other side of the room we shared on the second floor at 4060 W. 210th St. in Fairview Park, Ohio. I had kept him up late the night before with my typical seven-year-old's ruminations about life's big issues, like, does God really know the number of hairs on my head and if pulling one out would help get his attention regarding my Christmas prayer requests?

Denny sat upright as I shook him harder and told him we were going to check on the Christmas presents. His hair stuck straight up from the back of his head like Alfalfa's of the Little

Rascals as was its constant condition until he got really hand-some in his junior year of high school. Our slippers cushioned the sound of our stealthy descent past our older sister Lynn's bedroom, to the first-floor hallway just ten feet from where Mom and Dad slept together in their big double bed. Careful not to dis-turb the babies, David and Steve, asleep in the nursery down the hall, we turned left in the soft darkness and, without turning on the lights, crept over the linoleum kitchen floor, down the back stairs, past the door to the back porches and then down the base-ment stairs.

At the landing, the smell of freshly washed clothes wafted from the laundry room to our left where Mom spent a third of her life. Straight ahead was the door to Dad's basement office where he spent two thirds of his days working on the Orange Line Telephone Directory. But to the right, was the room of won-ders, the family Christmas tree and presents.

With full abandon now, Denny reached up to his full five-year-old height and switched on the light in the recreation room. Eight hours earlier we had been there decorating the Christmas tree and hanging our stockings on the mantle over the brick fireplace, but now everything looked so different. The tree trunk was completely blocked by presents that were all stacked high and close because the normal space available for presents for the seven of us in the family was now reduced by something so won-derful, I was struck speechless. Railroad tracks. Not the childish plastic tracks for a little kid's wind-up train. No. The big, heavy-gauge, three-rail steel tracks for a Lionel "Silver Bullet" passen-ger train. And there it was with the massive engine and four long, passenger cars gleaming in streamlined chrome.

I had asked for a train. I begged for a train. I went for broke and said no to all other gift suggestions. Mom didn't understand. She could not comprehend how essential an electric train was for a young boy. Dad knew. The transformer and control dial were hooked up and begged to be tested. No doubt, Dad gave that sleek beauty a few runs around the Christmas tree just to test his own skills at keeping her on the tracks. I knew what to do because a friend of mine let me operate his Lionel freight train. But his workhorse was no match for this sculptured racehorse.

I flipped the switch to "ON," watched the indicator light glow a brilliant red, and felt the excitement build as the powerful transformer began to heat up. Denny squatted at my side, taking it all in. "You sure we should start it up? What if they hear us?" I completely ignored him, driven by the urge to experience the thrill of my own train. Hand on the throttle, I slowly turned the dial clockwise and felt the minute clicks as it moved across the settings. The headlight, boldly centered on the great central tank of the steam engine, began to glow with a faint yellow light that reflected off the metallic wrapping paper like light off a wet canyon wall. Each of the four passenger cars lit up from the inside, showing off the big picture windows that flanked the sides. A humming grew in the engine and the crankshafts began their movements back and forth with the first turning of the drive wheels.

I advanced the throttle several more clicks and watched her respond to my wish. She was picking up speed now and beginning to strain against the curvature of the track. "Wow!" cried Denny. "Look at it go!" The headlight swept its beam around the room and illuminated the back wall, then flashed off the steel legs of the bar stools. Faster! More clicks to the right and I could feel the warmth of that transformer pumping out the power. I smelled something. Something oily. Not unpleasant, it had a sort of sweet, cooked smell that reminded me of warm syrup or the faint odor after a summer lightning storm. At three-quarter throttle, she careened around the tree, lights blazing and wheels making miniature screams as they clawed at the tracks on the tight continuous turn. I didn't know how it hung on, but I didn't dare try any more power. I was lost in the sheer glory of the moment.

Then a wave of fear came over me that we were pushing the limits of risk and could be caught. "Let's go!" Denny said nervously, echoing my feelings. I scaled back the throttle and watched the process reverse itself. My Silver Bullet slowed its breakneck pace to a crawl and creaked to a stop. A moment later the lights dimmed to a dull golden glow and went out as I dialed it down. I imagined I shared the same satisfied release the engineer of the real Silver Bullet felt after completing an unscheduled run at near top speed. We left quickly, remembering to turn out the light as we scampered back to the safety of our bedroom accompanied only by the slight whooshing sounds of our flannel PJs.

Sleep came easy and so did dreams of what it would feel like to be small enough to look out from the engine room of my most wonderful toy. I was awakened abruptly by my father bellowing my name. I came to the landing and saw him at the bottom of the stairs. His wavy black hair flopped slightly over the thick black eyebrows that formed roofs for brooding eyes that fiercely glowered at me. "Come with me, young man!" he ordered and turned towards the basement stairs. As I hurried after him, the wondrous train memory of just a few hours earlier came to mind, but it was immediately tainted by a threatening cloud of doom. Down the stairs we went, only this time no reassuring smell of fresh laundry greeted me, only that ever-thickening sweet smell. The recreation room looked different when Dad turned on the light. The room was clouded in a thick soup of gray smoke that oozed that same smell as Dad grabbed my little hand and dragged me in.

"You came down and played with your train before Christmas, didn't you?"

"Y-y-y-yes-s-s," I meekly admitted. What would have been the point of lying? I feared I had violated one of the Ten Commandments: "Thou shalt not have premature enjoyment." "Well," he continued in his best authoritarian voice, "you left it on and burned out the transformer. You could have burnt the house down. It goes back in the box right now, and you will never get a new one."

Unmoved by my tears, he handed me a large cardboard box and began to help me disassemble the magical thing that had brought me such joy and now an equivalent amount of pain.

I don't know what put more of a damper on that Christmas, my despondent mood or that ever-present, penetrating smell. Ozone, I later learned. It happened when the transformer gave up after struggling for hours to convert 120 volts into heat and dissipate it. Defeated, it just allowed its insides to be fried and then shorted out with a cloud of ozone-rich smoke.

Dad must have thought I learned my lesson. Two days later he gave me an additional present. A new transformer. We both returned to the basement with the box of parts and set up the track, this time in the middle of the room so nothing could impede our enjoyment of the Silver Bullet.

Moscow Nights

My dad could play wonderful tenths. His big left hand could reach an impossible length on the family's mahogany Janssen piano. His fingers seemed to unhinge like a snake's jaw to embrace two notes, ten tones apart at the far low end of the eighty-eights, then they would perform a spread-eagled walk up the keys. Sometimes he'd rock the two notes to accentuate the rhythm while always keeping a steady beat to hold the piece together. On the offbeat, his right hand, with a mind of its own, would start up the melody with a simple and clear theme at first, and then he would fill out the bare swing tones with sharps and flats that added rich color and a dash of jazzy spice.

As a novice pianist, I recognized only the major and minor chords in the basic keys like C, D, F and G. Dad loved the less-used keys like E-flat and A-flat. Diminished, sevenths, major sevenths, augmented, sixths, ninths and tenths were the chords he liked best, I later realized. His love of playing inspired me to explore the same style of picking out the melody and the chords by ear, and then play them in a personal style. On many nights, the entire family gathered around the piano to play together, with Dad, Lynn, David, and me taking turns at the keys.

Dad would accompany his own whispery soft singing and whistling of tunes, a nostalgic passport that took him back to the war years. They often went together—a few tunes on the piano in his inimitable style followed by a retelling of his adventures. I never tired of the stories. He served in the US Marine Corps both stateside and on the Pacific Island of Guam. Although trained to re-arm aircraft, his real talent was with recruiting, training, and deploying men for his orchestra. Although he didn't read music, he had the gumption to organize a small band while stationed in California, and then build it into a first-class orchestra that played for all kinds of military affairs. He even used his considerable powers of persuasion to have the entire orchestra shipped to Guam with him. Playing with J.B. could really get you places in those days.

A decade after the war was over and the orchestra broke up, Dad tried to start another band—this one stationed in the basement of our house on Cleveland's W. 210th St. "Hey, you kids want to have some fun?" he asked to the collection of kids hanging out there. Employing that same expertise in recognizing and motivating musical talent, he convinced us to gather our instruments while he flipped through one of my older sister Lynn's music books for an appropriate beginning piece.

My brother Denny ran to get the giant accordion he was so proud of, and our next-door neighbor, Axel, a recent emigrant from then West Germany, ran home for his father's saxophone. Neighbor Greg found two makeshift drumsticks and arranged our vinyl bar stools to serve as drumheads. At first, I seated myself at the tinny sounding practice piano we kept in the basement, but Dad brought Lynn down so I gladly relinquished the seat to the family's most accomplished musician. I grabbed the Clavietta, a two-and-a-half-octave keyboard that you blew through for an accordion-like sound.

We were ready with a five-piece band, but soon discovered Axle's saxophone was a B-flat instrument. Since he couldn't play it anyway, it didn't really matter. Dad told him he would find some notes for him to play. With the same confidence that got him half-way around the globe in World War Two, Dad declared we would play a sprite little tune called "Moscow Nights." Denny and I gathered around Lynn at the piano as Dad directed her to run through the piece slowly so we all could hear how it sounded. It was written in an exotic minor key with interesting chord progressions. At age seven, I wasn't sure where Moscow was, but the song sure made its nights sound intriguing.

With some gentle coaching from Dad, we were able to strike some of the right notes within a beat or two of each other. Even Axel successfully blasted out a few harmonic tones on his dad's raspy brass horn. Lynn's steady playing, and Greg's enthusiastic drumming constituted the positive side. To my untrained ears, I really thought we were playing the song, or at least the song was there somewhere camouflaged amidst the jungle of notes. Dad, however, had this grimace on his face. He suggested we practice the piece while he went upstairs for a break. Practice did not go well. Without Dad's guiding presence, we deteriorated quickly from discord, through total disarray, and settled on dissonance. Dad returned about a half hour later to see how we had progressed. "All right now, let's hear it from the top, and slow it down. Savvy?" But even Lynn's admirable perseverance could not redeem the piece—now accompanied by an all-male drum corps. Dad surrendered and retreated upstairs. Even an ex-Marine could not help us.

Four decades hence, both the Clavietta and the Janssen sit proudly in our living room. However, no one has dared play "Moscow Nights" on them since that day.

Firsts

In 1965, my family took the one major vacation of my youth. It's not that we couldn't afford vacations. I think my parents waited eighteen years after starting a family for the big trip because they were too busy obeying the Pope and producing new Catholics every 18-24 months (eight kids in fourteen years). Plus, they worked very hard to develop the first family business. Nearly four decades later, the summer of 1965 still looms in the memories of us surviving kids.

Mom and Dad bought an 8-by-35-foot Mustang travel trailer to pull behind the Country Squire station wagon. Everything in the trailer converted into a bed to sleep the nine of us. We drove it nearly six thousand miles over five weeks from Cleveland to San Francisco, and then to the Southwest and home again. It was trip packed with "firsts:" First time to see the wonders of the great American West, its incredible national parks, deserts, glaciers, and rushing rivers. There was Disneyland, killer heat, an incredible dust storm, full sky "heat" lightening, and my first infatuation with a girl and kiss (but that's another story).

This story centers on my first casino. Dad hit the jackpot the same afternoon we pulled into Los Vegas at the Golden Nugget Casino. He decided to splurge and bought four tickets for a dinner theater show for the outrageous sum of $38 and change. Back at the KOA trailer park, Denny and David pulled babysitting duty over the little ones, Steve, Sally, and Joe. The show's sixteen-and-older requirement excluded the younger kids—and me too—but nobody stopped us as Lynn and I returned to the Golden Nugget with Mom and Dad.

As we walked through the gaming rooms to the dinner theater, the opulence was overpowering and the drone of the machines and their frenetic gamblers was hypnotic. A uniformed waiter seated us in a semicircular booth where we could all view the curtained stage. I was fifteen at the time and on summer vacation from Borromeo Seminary where I was preparing for an ascetic life as a priest. The future I pictured mimicked the romantic stories of the saints. It was to be one of austere poverty but enriched by the rapture of serving my fellow man. Then came food so rich and wonderful I began to question the wisdom of my holy quest.

After gorging on our feast, with our dishes removed and coffee and drinks served by our uniformed waiter, the lights dimmed for the start of the show, "Orpheus and the Underworld." I was vaguely familiar with the ancient myth from my Latin classes. Something about ancient gods who took occasional vacations as mortals to experience the human joys and hungers until they had to return to their regular roles as fickle rulers of the universe. I was not familiar with the theater troupe that presented the show, the "Follies de Paris."

A drum roll silenced the audience and the lights faded to black while the huge curtain opened. An intense spotlight flashed on and washed a person who stood at center stage with head slumped down, dressed entirely in black from a top hat to a cape that cascaded onto the stage. I could just make out a line of human figures behind that stretched the width of the stage. As blue and red floor lights came up, I saw that the line of figures were showgirls dressed in skimpy white costumes who stood with their backs to the audience. My interest grew even knowing my future had celibacy as a defining characteristic. When the figure in black slowly looked up, I saw her lovely face. She raised her arms and flared the black cape open like the slow-motion nature film of a falcon preparing for flight. Meanwhile, the line of showgirls turned in unison to face their audience.

"Oh my God!" Mom cried out. "This is a topless show!? Bernie, what the hell were you thinking?"

"Wow," I thought, "do I have a great dad or what?"

We both hit the jackpot that night.

Strike Up The Band

I hung up the phone in the Indiana Turnpike rest stop with my sister-in-law's words still echoing in my ears: "Your dad's cardiologist said his liver and gall bladder have stopped functioning. He said one of the lobes of his lung is down completely and the other is only at fifty percent of normal with the help of oxygen. His bladder shut down and his heart is so damaged from congestive heart failure, it's a miracle he's hanging on. Michael, the doctor said the only major organ that's working is his brain."

Cynthia, our daughter, Jessica, and I were racing to the hospital in my former hometown of Cleveland. It was the spring of 1997 and I feared it would be my dad's last. He said he really wanted to live to see eighty but I wasn't sure he'd last long enough for us to get to the hospital, much less the six months to that birthday. As Cynthia drove, I pecked away at a memoir of my war experiences on the laptop. I felt a deep urge to share some of my writing with him.

We found him lying in a private room in St. John's Hospital, sheet pulled up mid chest. Tubes and wires snaked out from under the sheet and from his arms, nose, and mouth. They were connected to the surrounding mechanical marvels of medicine that whirred, bubbled, and beeped with sounds of postponed death. My father looked shrunken and pale. The flabby skin on his arms looked camouflaged with the deep reds, blues, and sickly greens of bruises caused by the hourly need to insert needles for adding or subtracting fluids.

A long time passed before his eyelids opened, heavy with dark folds of loose chicken-like skin, and his head moved slightly with recognition of our presence. I patted his hand, careful not to disturb the IV taped nearby. Bending over, I said hi, and gave him a kiss on his blotchy forehead. Cynthia and Jessica followed in kind and we left a few minutes later when Dad fell back to sleep.

Over the next few days, my dad pulled off a near-miraculous recovery, a feat he would repeat two additional times over the next two years. My father was tough. He was a child of the Great Depression. This had a crucial effect on his philosophy of life. The pervasive national feeling of desperation and ever-immanent poverty had the effect of elevating material wealth and financial independence to the level of godliness. His father was a successful businessman who weathered the Depression through lots of hard work, frugality, and high expectations of those who worked for him. He had business acumen and did not ask for any handouts. Dad aspired to and achieved these same virtues. From the time he left home after high school graduation to be a traveling salesman to when he died, he never worked for anyone else. The exception was his stint in the Marines. Even here, he achieved a high degree of autonomy as a bandleader and manager of a serviceman's bar on Guam.

The idea for his own publishing business hatched on Guam. After the war, he began to build his empire. First by taking a beautiful and enthralled woman off a dirt-poor Mississippi farm and make her his wife, and then by making babies, lots of them, eight in all. He built several small businesses that supported this large family at the level of middle-class luxury.

I don't think Dad had very much interest in accumulating lots of goods and services as a striving businessman. However, money was his primary gauge of success, not what money could buy. If he couldn't make money at something, he wasn't interested in it. He offered no free handouts to his offspring. All assistance had financial or philosophical strings attached. I think that Dad believed that God blessed good people with financial success and cursed bad people with poverty.

On a bright morning when he was feeling much better and had a full night's sleep with few interruptions from the hospital staff, we had a chance to visit alone and I had my opportunity to tell him about my memoir. "Dad, I've been writing about my experiences in Vietnam and I hoped you might want to hear some of it." "Funny you should mention war stories, Son," he answered. "I was just telling the nurse about Santa Barbara. Oh yeah, I'd like to hear your story," he added reassuringly. But then he turned away, stared at the ceiling and continued, "You know, it's amazing to me. I can't remember what I had for breakfast but I can remember World War Two like the movie was still showing in my head. I was just telling this nurse how we used to perform for the servicemen at the El Paseo."

Dad repeated the stories of when he was a Marine stationed during the War in Santa Barbara, near San Diego. With a happy gleam in his near-blind eyes, he talked fondly of the small band he formed while assigned to aircraft ordinance at the nearby Marine Corps Air Station. He told how his CO took a liking to him and his "Combo," as he called it, and helped him formalize it into a full Marine Corps orchestra that played for civic and military functions throughout the Santa Barbara area. "We played two nights a week at the Elks Club for the servicemen and occasionally at the country club too. Used to be able to play golf for free there." Dad went on about later running the Enlisted Men's club on Guam, the "Slop Chute;" stories I never tired of hearing.

I thought back on the countless times I enjoyed his collection of scalloped-edge, black and white photos of those war years. My father in his late 20s, standing proudly in Marine khakis in front of his thirty-piece orchestra with raven-black hair flopping out from under a raked hat, baton in hand. Dad in a semi-circular booth of smiling couples with a table stocked with drinks, hands clasping cigarettes, and faces beaming with smiles. Dad with his arms encircling the waists of two buxom showgirls. The shot of Dad, in front of his bar at the Slop Chute shaking hands with a much taller fellow Kentuckian, Victor Mature, who went on to make sixty Hollywood movies. Old pictures of a much younger man, strikingly handsome, smiling, gregarious, creative, confident and accomplished.

We both wore the uniform in service to our country. This was a relationship bridge that, unique among my siblings, I shared with him.

Dad added that his CO at Santa Barbara told him once that boosting the morale of the troops was an essential contribution to the war effort. He summed up his wartime experience with the comment, "I guess I went through the war with a beer in one hand and a baton in the other helping the fighting men fight."

Turning back to me, he said, "Guess Vietnam was a little different, huh, Son." I took his comment as an invitation to begin. Using my laptop computer, I began reading the chapter in the book I published four years later titled, "A Terrible Beauty: Operation Durham Peak in the Que Son Mountains." Since this chapter most resembled a straightforward war story, I thought it would be appropriate. He seemed very interested in the computer and confused by the story. Undeterred, I continued but before long, I heard him begin to snore. I put down the laptop and placed my hand on his. Without opening his eyes, he concluded the session by saying in a voice that was a shrunken imitation of the god-like voice that raised me as a boy, "Vietnam was very different."

"Bye, Dad. I'll come back later. Love you."

"Bye, Son."

I left satisfied.

13. KEEP ON SINGING

I t's the third Thursday of the month. I park the Sienna van in the drop-off circle at the main entrance to the Minnesota Veterans Home, activate the flashers, and make two trips to stage my equipment in the lobby. The receptionist, Kay, assures me she will keep an eye on it while I move the van to the main parking lot. Briefcase over one shoulder, mic stand strapped over the other, I carry one of the two guitars I brought through the building's impressive, three-story rotunda and past the serene-looking chapel and the small history museum and store. Along the way to the fourth floor's Memory Care Unit, I pause to take in the beauty of the closet-sized cage that teems with flitting little birds. Everywhere are staff, family caretakers, visitors, and other volunteers like me. A woman with a therapy dog coming the other way pauses to say hello and, "Thank you for your service." I'm donning a hat that I only wear here at the Veterans Home. Its gaudy embroidered message shouts that I served with the Marines in Vietnam. It's a bridge to the veterans I've come to entertain.

I will use the same song set here in the Memory Care Unit that I played earlier in the week at two other facilities at the Veterans Home, the residence building for veterans who do not need intensive nursing care, and the Adult Day Center. My friend, Jim Kurtz,[25] joined me for both of those other performances to tell jokes in between my songs. Music and mirth, that's our schtick for the vets in those two other facilities. He says his mission in life, now that he's retired, is to affirm the goodness in everyone he meets. "We all need to hear that we matter and are valued." When saying goodbye, he typically adds a sincere, "Thank you for all that you do." We met playing pickleball at the YMCA two years ago. He always had a joke that he delivered with whatever convincing Norwegian, Irish, British, or Russian accent the joke demanded. He'd have all the guys in the locker room laughing. So now, at the Veterans Home, he's added standup comedy to his good-will mission.

Last month, he told a joke about a guy who was able to get the very last ticket to the Superbowl, which was held in Minneapolis in 2018. His seat was the worst one sold, located at the top of the nose-bleed section far from the action. Half an hour into the game, he sees an empty seat, ten rows up from the 50-yard line, and decides to check it out. He asks an old man in an adjacent seat whether the vacant one is available. "Well you see," the man explains, "It was my wife's seat but she died. But you can sit there." The guy thanks the old man as he sits down and then says, "I've gotta' ask you, couldn't you have given the ticket to another family member or a friend?" "No," the old man says. "They're all at the funeral."

Jim is convinced that, before he delivers his best jokes, he needs one or two "groaners," puns or one-liners in the style of Rodney Dangerfield. He explained that the vets want to laugh and the groaners make them hungrier for a good joke. Nick is one of our favorites at the Adult Day Center. He sits in the front row and, good joke or bad, he often exclaims "Oh, brother!" and triggers a secondary round of laughter. I invite ideas for songs. For example, Richard, suggested Frank Sinatra's macho, signature song "My Way." "Only if you will sing it with me," I challenged him. Many times, Richard and I have crooned the song together, Las Vegas style, for the group.

"Oh, brother!"

Jim and I have listened to the stories from the vets in the residence building and the Adult Day Center: The Special Forces vet who had completed more than forty parachute jumps, and another paratrooper who was wounded in World War Two's Battle of the Bulge. The three sailors who saw combat off the coast of Vietnam on board the aircraft carrier, *USS Hancock*, and the guided missile cruisers, *USS Boston* and the *USS Buchanan*. We listened as Steve stated he had served for twelve years in Air Force intelligence but refused to say anything more about his experiences. "I'm not permitted to say." When I asked about his work after leaving the service, he gave the same answer. I call him, "Steve, the Man of Mystery."

In contrast, Peter is a non-stop story teller. He said he was a Navy Corpsman and a helicopter crew member in Vietnam. With details that included place names, specific dates, and military unit names, he described his role as a chopper crewman for the 1990 movie, *Air America*, about the CIA's operations in Laos during the Vietnam War. "Oh sure," he answered to a question I asked with no small hint of skepticism. "I met Mel Gibson and Robert Downey Jr." Twice, Peter told me that he was "knighted as the Queen's cousin," and both times, he substantiated this story with detailed history and lineage references while his tone gradually took on a British accent. I really don't care whether the stories are fully or partially true, or just the product of a smart but delusional mind. He's a fascinating person. I'm there to entertain; not to judge.

I was delighted to meet Mark at the residence and learn that we both served as grunts in Vietnam with the First Marines during the same period, only in different regiments. We both fought the North Vietnamese Army in the jungles and the Que Son mountains on Operation Durham Peak. Turns out that Mark and I met on July 20, 2019, exactly fifty years after the first moonwalk. Although people at least my age still remember that day with as much clarity as JFK's assassination, I first heard about this momentous event the day I left Vietnam *eight months* later. Mark burst into laughter when I recounted this experience. He had a similar story. Both of us had honed similar survival strategies of ignoring the rest of *The World* in order to maintain a laser focus on keeping ourselves and our fellow Marines alive.

As the automatic door to the Memory Care Unit opens, soft music mixes with the faint smell from adult diapers doing their job. I walk between a big screen TV playing an episode of *Bonanza* with the sound off and a half dozen old men sleeping, slumped and slack jawed in lounge chairs on wheels. Among them is my dear friend, Jack. A near-fatal stroke has reduced his life of vigorous health and activism with Veterans For Peace to that of an invalid.

Becky, the unit's recreation director, attends to the man I call "Mr. Hey." She sees me, waves hello, and I stage my first load under one of the eight-foot windows that flood the room with warm morning sunlight. I repeat the process with my second load from the lobby carrying my other guitar, amplifier, and music stand. I have twenty minutes to set it all up, pee, and get a cup of hot tea for my vocal cords.

I have prepared a dozen songs from my coming-of-age period in the late 60s and early 70s for the twenty-five men Becky has wheeled into position in front of me. Most appear to still be asleep. I introduce myself as a fellow veteran and begin belting out "With a Little Help From My Friends," trying to channel Joe Cocker's interpretation of the Beatles song. "What would you do if I sang out of tune? Would you stand up and walk out on me?" I know there is little chance of that actually happening with this captive audience. Before I sing the Beatles' "A Day In the Life," I give a brief explanation of the song's obscure lyrics and how it's a fusion of two completely different musical ideas. Midway through, "Mr. Hey" begins his loud chant from the back of the room: "Hey! Hey! Hey! Hey!" I sing closer to the mic as Becky wheels him to a different room on the floor.

I move on to "Fakin' It" and "American Tune" by Paul Simon, and then "Dream of Me," made famous by the Mommas and Papas. Three caregiving wives are also in the audience plus other staff members who drift in and out, tending to individual veterans or just listening. I see some heads bob with the music, some feet tap, some hands wave. For most, there is no reaction whatsoever, but it doesn't matter. Becky applauds loudly after every song along with the wives and other staff. A couple of the veterans join them haltingly. One veteran to my left waves both hands enthusiastically with a broad smile on his face.

I hold up my guitar for all to see, a Gibson J45 Dreadnaught that I bought with the $187 I requested from my parents for my high school graduation in 1966. I describe, actually with some degree of pride, how a falling lamp gouged its face; how my friend's wife stepped on it and cracked the body; and how it survived a winter hitchhiking trip to New Orleans. The penultimate story is how my cousin set it on fire. He said he could take care of a slight warping of the body by heating it with an iron. He didn't know that in 1966, Gibson used a nitro-cellulose lacquer finish that was highly flammable. He did his best to refinish it, but the affected area remains clearly visible like an iron-shaped birthmark.

I bang out an E chord, the best sounding chord on any quality guitar, and it reverberates throughout the room. This vintage guitar with its proud scars produces a resonating sound, as rich and full as a cello's, that even its current model, priced at $2,400, can't match.

Next, I switch to my Barkley twelve-string to play Joni Mitchell's "Chelsea Morning," I explain the guitar's extra strings and the chromatic tuning for the song. I know the staff and wives may be comprehending all of this but probably no one else —but it doesn't matter.

After forty minutes of performing, I ask Becky to pass out the sing-along booklets I brought and ask for requests. They have thirty-three songs to choose from, and Becky asks for "Leaving On a Jet Plane" by John Denver. We get through the first verse and I notice that one of the men off to my right in the front row is crawling on his hands and knees towards me. I stop playing and bring it to Becky's attention. "No problem, Michael," she says calmly. "You can keep singing." Becky brings the man to his feet and they dance to the music. I struggle to hold back soft tears—and keep on singing.

APPENDIX

Wisdom from the Experts

Additional Reading

This is for readers who want additional information from the writers who helped me the most:

Ken Druck, Ph.D. and James C. Simmons, authors of *The Secrets Men Keep: Breaking the Silence Barrier*, write about the "father hole" I described in Chapter 5:

> Initially, we all want to love and to be loved by our father. When his love for us is withdrawn, found to be highly conditional, fades away, is lost, or simply has never been made available to us, we respond in turn by cutting off our expression of love for him. We close our hearts to our father. We deny that we still have a need for his love and approval. But we still carry around, buried secretly inside us, the child we once were who wanted so desperately his father's love. Unconscious, we still seek it—in success, wealth, status, or the approval of other men.[26]

In his book, *I Don't Want to Talk about It*, Terrence Real provides a synopsis of what it means to be a father, a man, and a more complete person:

> Traditional masculinity deprives men the experience of community. Those who fear subjugation have limited repertoires of service. But service is the appropriate central organizing force of manhood. When the critical question concerns what one is going to get, a man is living in a boy's world. Beyond a certain point in a man's life, if he is to remain truly vital, he needs to be actively engaged in devotion to something other than his own success and happiness. The word *discipline* derives from the same root as *disciple*. Discipline means, "to place one-

self in the service of." Discipline is a form of devotion. A grown man with nothing to devote himself to is a man who is sick at heart.

What a great many men in this culture choose to serve is their own reflected value, which they often believe serves the needs of their family, even while their families may be crying out for something different from them .... This culture, with its reliance on performance-based esteem, gives men few models for healthy sacrifice ... . Yet it is the placing of oneself at the service of a larger context that drives a man deep into his own growth and fullest potential ... to live for something beyond performance, kudos, and acquisition.[27]

The book by Terry Kellogg, M.A. and Marvel Harrison Kellogg, Ph.D. *Broken Toys Broken Dreams: Understanding and Healing Codependency*, lists the most common sources of sanctuary betrayal. The first four sources were especially rampant in the Orange household (the following are excerpts):

1. **Inconsistency and unpredictability:** When our guardians of family members are addicted, mentally ill or chronically stressed, we never know how they will respond or what will happen.
2. **Authority intrusion:** This includes physical, sexual, spiritual, emotional and intellectual violations ... . Violence is a violation of self, boundaries, body, spirit, mind, space, property or other properties. Over-control, manipulation, seduction, and perfection are also intrusions.
3. **Authority detachment:** Unavailability, neglect, distancing, passive aggressive postures are sources of hurt and stress. Abandonment of survival figures because of illness, inability to support, running away, death or divorce can be

experienced as life threatening to children and some adults.

4. **Authority discord:** When survival figures are distant, cold, angry, fighting or unavailable to each other, the foundation of the system is shaky and survival feels threatened. Woody Allen once said the biggest fight we have in our life is our fight with our parents. This is not true for many of us—the biggest fight we have is our parents' fight with each other.

5. **Reality distortion and high denial:** This is when we are not told what is going on around us and/or what we are told is not true. In actuality at some level we really always know what is going on but when we are told something different or something is denied we feel at loose ends, disconnected and a bit 'crazy.' Then we lose our ability to trust our instincts, intuition and feeling. We lose our inner guidance systems.[28]

In his book, *Bradshaw on: The Family. A New Way of Creating Solid Self Esteem*, John Bradshaw describes patriarchal parenting rules as a "poisonous pedagogy" that "exalts obedience as its highest value. Following obedience are orderliness, cleanliness, and the control of emotions and desires. Children are considered 'good' when they think and behave the way they are taught to think and behave."

A crucial result of this monarchial rearing, as Bradshaw calls it, and the practice of using toxic shame to suppress normal childhood behaviors is the loss of solid self-esteem and the development of a false self. Bradshaw writes, "Children raised by patriarchal parenting rules quickly learn that the way to get love is to give up their authentic self and develop a self that meets the demands of blind obedience and duty. When the core of self is covered up with a false self, true self-love and self-esteem are impossible."

Very importantly, Bradshaw points out that parents were causing this damage to their children *unknowingly* or *unintentionally.* "I tried to make it clear," he explains when he is talking to parents, "that it is not a matter of blame. Our parents did the best they could within the limits of their own awareness. Monarchial child rearing is seen as abusive only when our consciousness shifts toward a deeper internalization of democracy." Bradshaw explains that, because parents who never had their childhood needs met are themselves still needy, "They therefore cannot give to their children what they do not have themselves."

Bradshaw clearly describes the psychological mechanisms at work here (as did Terrence Real) and it warrants considerable attention (italics are in the original):

> The magical part of the child's thinking *deifies the parents* ... . This magical idealization serves to protect the child from the terrors of the night, which are about abandonment and, to the child, death. The protective deification of the parents, this magical idealization, also creates a potential for a shame-binding predicament for the child.
>
> For example, if the parents are abusive and hurt the child through physical, sexual, emotional or mental pain, the child will assume the blame and make himself bad in order to keep the all-powerful parental protection. For a child at this stage, realizing the inadequacies of parents would produce unbearable anxiety ... .
>
> Since no mother, father or other parenting person is perfect, all humans develop this [magical idealization] to some degree. In fact, growing up and leaving home involves the overcoming of this illusion of connection and protection. Growing up means accepting our fundamental aloneness.[29]

Ironically, the more a person has been emotionally deprived, the stronger their "magical idealization," according to Bradshaw. "Idealizing parents also extends to the way they raised you." Bradshaw continues:

> The child parents himself the way he was parented. If the child got shamed for feeling angry, sad, or sexual, he will shame himself each time he feels angry, sad, or sexual ... . The inner self-rupture is so painful, the child develops a 'false self.' This false self manifests in a mask or rigid role that is determined both by culture and the family system's need for balance. Over time the child identifies with the false self and is largely unconscious of his own true feelings, needs, and wants. The shame is internalized. Shame is no longer a feeling; it is an identity. The real self has withdrawn from conscious contact and therefore cannot be the object of his esteem.
>
> Even after the magical period passes, around the age of eight, and the child moves into a more logical way of thinking, nature continues to provide an egocentric idealization of the parents ... . [T]he logical child will remain egocentric and undifferentiated until early puberty. Only then will he have the capacity for other-centered love and understanding.[30]

Bradshaw explains that the child's false shame-based self and model of their idealized family is "cast in bronze" to the degree that even when new information is self-evident, they will warp it to fit their mental and emotional model.

This leads to loss of one's true self. "To be de-selfed," he writes, "is to have one's self-esteem severely damaged." This is a major cause of the rage that dominates our world. "The rage is either directed against strangers in crimes of violence, or it is directed against ourselves as the shame that fuels our addictions."

Bradshaw returns to this last theme regarding the damage to society caused by dysfunctional families and the compulsive behaviors they spawn. "Most of our present human dysfunction can be described by the term compulsivity. Violence, sexual disorders, emotional and religious addictions are the ills that destroy people's lives."

Bradshaw writes about the role of emotions (he refers to them as "e-motions") and the results of their repression. "[E-motions] are energies in motion. If they are not expressed, the energy is repressed. As energy, it has to go somewhere. Emotional energy moves us. We are moved to tears when we have lost something dear to us.

In *Buddha's Brain: The Practical Neuroscience of Happiness, Love, and Wisdom*, doctors Rick Hanson and Richard Mendius write, "Growing up, many of us felt let down by people who should have been better protectors. The deepest upsets are often not with those who harmed you but with the people who didn't prevent it—they're the ones you probably had the strongest attachment bonds to and thus felt most let down by. So, it's understandable if your inner protector is not as strong as it could be."[31]

Bradshaw describes how alcoholism is an all-pervasive, time-consuming addiction that prevents the alcoholic from attending to their child-rearing responsibilities. "Alcoholic parents, no matter how good their intentions, physically abandon their children ... . Abandonment sets up compulsivity. Since the children need their parents all of the time, and since they do not get their needs met, they grow up looking and talking like adults, but having within them an insatiable little child who never got his or her needs met. They have an inner emptiness, and this drives their compulsivity. They look for *more and more love*, attention, praise, booze, money, etc."

And then there are the roles we played as kids. Again, Bradshaw nails it with a perfect description of the roles my siblings and I assumed as children in our dysfunctional family (Bradshaw capitalizes the roles "to signify their rigidity"):

In chronically dysfunctional families, the family members are selectively cut off from many of their feelings and are in rigid role performances … . They function to keep the family system in balance. If Dad is a workaholic and never home, one of the children will become Mom's Emotional Spouse since the system needs a marriage for balance. In an alcoholic family, one child will be a Hero or Heroine because the family system needs some dignity. If the family system has no warmth, one child will become the Emotional Caretaker and be warm and loving to everyone. If the system is ravaged with unexpressed anger and pain, one child will become the Scapegoat and act out all of the anger and pain … .

In addition to balancing the chronically dysfunctional family, rigid roles are the false selves that shame-based family members use in order to have a sense of control over the distress the family is experiencing.[32]

Therapist, Robert Burney, compares the source and effects of PTSD from wartime trauma to childhood trauma in his book, *Codependence: The Dance of Wounded Souls*:

In a war, soldiers have to deny what it feels like to see friends killed and maimed; what it feels like to kill other human beings and have them attempting to kill you. … The stress caused by the trauma … eventually surfaces in ways which produce new trauma—anxiety, alcohol and drug abuse, nightmares, uncontrollable rage, inability to maintain relationships, inability to hold jobs, suicide, etc.

Instead of blood and death (although some do experience blood and death literally), what happened to us as children was spiritual death and emotional maiming, mental torture and physical violation … . We were forced to deny our feelings about what we were experiencing and seeing and sensing. We were forced to deny ourselves.

We grew up having to deny the emotional reality of parental alcoholism, addiction, mental illness, rage, violence, depression, abandonment, betrayal, deprivation, neglect, incest, etc. ... . [We grew up having to deny the emotional reality] of our parents fighting ...; of dad's ignoring us because of his workaholism and/or mom smothering us because she had no other identity than being a mother; of the abuse that one parent heaped on another . . .; the abuse we received from one of our parents while the other wouldn't defend us ... .

The war we were born into, the battlefield each of us grew up in, was not in some foreign country against some identified "enemy"—it was in the "homes" which were supposed to be our safe haven, with our parents whom we loved and trusted to take care of us ... . We experienced what is called "sanctuary trauma"—our safest place to be was not safe—and we experienced it on a daily basis for years and years ... . It was not a battlefield because our parents were wrong or bad. It was a battlefield because ... they were born into the middle of a war ... . Through being in recovery, we are helping to break the cycles of self-destructive behavior that have dictated human existence for thousands of years.[33]

RESOURCES

(Excerpts are from *from Shock Waves: A Practical Guide to Living With a Loved One's PTSD*, Cynthia Orange, 2010.)

About Ptsd

Post-traumatic stress disorder (PTSD): PTSD did not become an official diagnosis until 1980 when the American Psychiatric Association added it to its *Diagnostic and Statistical Manual of Mental Disorders.* In Civil War times, PTSD was called "soldier's heart" or "Da Costa's Syndrome," after Jacob Mendes Da Costa, the doctor who described an anxiety disorder with symptoms that mimicked heart disease. In World War I, doctors called it "shell shock," or "combat fatigue," and in World War Two it was also known as "gross stress reaction."

We can thank our Vietnam veterans and those who worked with them for getting PTSD accepted as a legitimate and diagnosable medical condition with long-lasting effects for the millions of people who experience serious trauma

A PTSD Diagnosis: To be diagnosed with PTSD, [the *Diagnostic and Statistical Manual of Mental Disorders* (DSM-IV)] specifies that a person must have been exposed to or have witnessed a traumatic event that involved actual or threatened death or serious injury to oneself or others. PTSD can also come from experiencing the unexpected or violent death, serious harm, or threat of harm, of someone close to you—family member or not. In a PTSD diagnosis, the person's response to the trauma involves intense fear, helplessness, or horror.

Duration: To be classified as PTSD, the traumatized person must have symptoms in three areas (reliving the trauma, avoidance and numbing, and hyper-arousal) and these symptoms–must last for more than one month. Those diagnosed with PTSD have difficulty going about their daily tasks because their relationships, jobs, and often every aspect of their lives are significantly affected by their symptoms.

Reliving the trauma: For people with PTSD, the traumatic event is re-experienced in one (or more) of the following ways:

- Recurrent or intrusive thoughts, images, or memories of the event.
- Nightmares or distressing dreams in which the trauma reemerges.
- Flashbacks, illusions, or hallucinations – all of which might cause the person to act or feel as if the traumatic event was still occurring, giving him or her a sense of re-living the experience.
- Mental or emotional anguish when something happens to trigger a recollection of some aspect of the event. For those who have lived or worked in war-torn areas, a car backfiring may sound like an explosion.
- Physical reactions when something triggers a memory of the trauma. For example, a person may react to a trigger with a stomach ache, a pounding heart or rapid breathing, sweating, or a severe headache.

Traumatic recollections might be triggered by an anniversary of the trauma; certain odors, sounds, textures, tastes, or sights; a medical procedure; an activity that replicates some aspect of the event; something that ignites fear like a close call on the freeway; certain places or spaces; a movie; a song, or by any event or stimulus.

Avoidance and numbing: People with PTSD adopt certain strategies to avoid places, objects, or people that remind them of the traumatic event. In a person diagnosed with PTSD, three (or more) of the following need to be present:

- An effort to avoid thoughts, feelings, or conversations associated with the trauma.
- An effort to avoid activities, places, or people that bring the trauma to mind.
- An inability to remember an important aspect of the trauma.
- A noticeable disinterest in doing things that were

enjoyable before the traumatic experience. (This reaction is often called "psychic numbing" or "emotional anesthesia.")

- A feeling of detachment or estrangement from others.
- Difficulty having or showing loving feelings or being intimate or sexual.
- A sense of a foreshortened future in which the person doesn't expect to have a career, marriage, children, or a normal life span.

Hyper-arousal: People with PTSD are anxious or on the alert, making it difficult for them to relax. In a PTSD diagnosis, two (or more) of the following symptoms are present:

- Difficulty falling or staying asleep (which could be due to nightmares about the trauma).
- Irritability or outbursts of anger.
- Difficulty concentrating on or completing tasks.
- Hyper-vigilance. This extreme sense of caution may sometimes be so intense it can resemble paranoia.
- Exaggerated startle response.

Acute, chronic, and delayed onset PTSD: DSM-IV refers to three distinctions under the PTSD umbrella that specify onset and duration of the symptoms:

- Acute PTSD refers to symptoms that last less than three months.
- Chronic PTSD refers to symptoms that last three months or longer.
- Delayed Onset PTSD refers to symptoms that did not appear until after six months or more have passed between the traumatic event and the onset of symptoms.

Getting Help

Call the National Suicide Prevention Lifeline at 1-800-273-TALK (8255) if you are feeling desperate, alone or hopeless. It is a free, 24-hour hotline available to anyone in suicidal crisis or emotional distress. Your call will be routed to the nearest crisis center to you. (Their Web site is www.suicidepreventionlifeline.org)

The hotline is staffed around the clock by trained counselors, and this service is free and confidential. In addition to helping you on the phone, they can provide information about mental health services in your area.

Who should call?
• Anyone who feels sad, hopeless, or suicidal
• Family and friends who are concerned about a loved one.
• Anyone interested in mental health treatment and service referrals.

Why should you call?
The Lifeline Network answers thousands of calls from people in emotional distress. There are many reasons for their calls. Please call for any of the following reasons:
• Suicidal thoughts
• Abuse or violence
• Information on suicide
• Economic problems
• Information on mental health
• Sexual orientation issues
• Substance abuse or addiction
• Physical illness
• To help a friend or loved one
• Loneliness
• Relationship problems
• Family problems

Books On Trauma And Ptsd

Catherall, Don R., Ph.D. Back From the Brink: *A Family Guide to Overcoming Traumatic Stress*. New York: Bantam Books, 1992.

Goulston, Mark., M.D. *Post-Traumatic Stress Disorder for Dummies*. Hoboken, N.J.: Wiley Publishing, 2008. A very helpful, easy-to-understand reference and overview for survivors of PTSD and their families.

National Center for PTSD (www.ptsd.va.gov) A great web site that offers helpful information about trauma and PTSD for survivors, families, and professionals.

National Child Traumatic Stress Network (www.nctsnet.org) Provides information and links on trauma and children and how to best help them.

National Institute of Mental Health PTSD site (www.nimh.nih.gov/health/topics/post-traumatic-stress-disorder-ptsd/index.shtml)
Good information on trauma and how adults and children can cope with violence and disasters. You can download a good booklet called "What Parents Can Do" at their Web site.

Mason, Patience H.C. *Recovering from the War: A Woman's Guide to Helping Your Vietnam Vet, Your Family, and Yourself*. New York: Viking Press, 1990. An informative resource for veterans and their families written by the wife of a Vietnam combat vet.

Matsakis, Aphrodite, Ph.D. *Vietnam Wives: Facing the Challenges of Life with Veterans Suffering Post-Traumatic Stress*. (Second Edition) Baltimore: Sidran Press, 1996. Although written for the families of veterans, I found this to be a very helpful and informative book for anyone dealing with the effects of trauma.

Post-Traumatic Gazette (www.patiencepress.com) Patience

Mason, wife of a Vietnam combat vet, provides tons of information about trauma and PTSD in newsletters and brochures—
many of which are free and easily downloaded.

PTSD forum (www.ptsdforum.org) Good site for cyber support
and information for survivors and families affected by trauma.

Shay, Jonathan Shay, M.D., Ph.D. *Achilles in Vietnam: Combat
Trauma and the Undoing of Character.* New York: Touchstone,
a division of Simon & Schuster, Inc., 1994. A fascinating book
that traces the history of PTSD and psychological effects of war
by comparing the experiences of soldiers in Homer's *Iliad* with
those of Vietnam veterans.

Orange, Cynthia L., *Shock Waves: A Practical Guide to Living with a
Loved One's PTSD.* Center City, Minnesota: Hazelden. 2010.

BIBLIOGRAPHY

Anderson, Kurt, *Fantasyland: How America Went Haywire, A 500-Year History*, New York: Random House, 2017.

Boyd, Andrew. *Daily Afflictions: The Agony of Being Connected to Everything.* New York: W.W. Norton & Company, Inc. 2002.

Bradshaw, John. *Bradshaw on: The Family. A New Way of Creating Solid Self Esteem.* Deerfield Beach, Florida: Health Communications, Inc. 1988.

Brinkley, Douglas, *Tour of Duty: John Kerry and the Vietnam War.* New York: Perennial, 2004.

Burney, Robert. *Codependence: The Dance of Wounded Souls.* Cambria, California: Joy to You & Me Enterprises. 1995.

Campbell, Joseph. *The Power of Myth with Bill Moyers.* New York: Doubleday, 1988.

Carroll, James. *Constantine's Sword: The Church and the Jews, A History.* New York: Mariner Books. 2002.

Druck, Ken, Ph.D. and James C. Simmons. *The Secrets Men Keep: Breaking the Silence Barrier.* Garden City, New York: Doubleday and Company, Inc. 1985.

Grossman, Dave, Lieutenant Colonel. *On Killing: The Psychological Cost of Learning to Kill in War and Society.* Boston: Little, Brown and Company, 1995.

Hanh, Thich Nhat. *Anger: Wisdom for Cooling the Flames.* New York: Riverhead Books. 2001.

_____*Living Buddha, Living Christ.* New York: Riverhead Books. 1995

_____*Peace is Every Step: The Path of Mindfulness in Daily Life.* New York: Bantam Books, 1991.

Hanson, Rick, Ph.D. and Richard Mendius, M.D. *Buddha's Brain:*

The Practical Neuroscience of Happiness, Love & Wisdom. Oakland, California: New Harbinger Publications, Inc. 2009.

Hedges, Chris. *War is a Force that Gives Us Meaning*. New York: Anchor Books. 2002.

Heschel, Rabbi Abraham Joshua. *God in Search of Man: A Philosophy of Judaism*. New York: Farrar, Straus and Giroux. 1955.

Howard, Lew. Introducing Ken Wilber: Concepts for an Evolving World. Bloomington, Indiana: Author House. 2005.

Kellogg, Terry, M.A. and Marvel Harrison Kellogg, Ph.D. *Broken Toys Broken Dreams: Understanding and Healing Codependency*. Lake Kiowa, Texas: B.R.A.T. Publishing. 1990.

Kornfield, Jack. *A Path with Heart: A Guide Through the Perils and Promises of Spiritual Life*. New York: Bantam Books, 1993.

Moore, Thomas. *Original Self: Living with Paradox and Originality*. New York: Perennial, an imprint of HarperCollins Publishers. 2001.

Orange, Cynthia. *Shock Waves: A Practical Guide to Living with a Loved One's PTSD*. Center City, Minnesota: Hazelden. 2010.

Orange, Cynthia. *Take Good Care: Finding Your Joy in Compassionate Caregiving*. Center City, Minnesota: Hazelden. 2017.

Orange, J. Michael. *Fire in the Hole: A Mortarman in Vietnam*. New York: Writers Club Press. 2001.

Real, Terrence. *I Don't Want to Talk About It: Overcoming the Secret Legacy of Male Depression*. New York: Simon and Schuster. 1997.

Rosen, Gerald M. *Posttraumatic Stress Disorder: Issues and Controversies*. New York: Wiley. 2004

Shay, Jonathan, M.D., Ph.D. *Achilles in Vietnam: Combat Trauma and the Undoing of Character*. New York: Scribner. 1994.

Storr, Anthony. *The Essential Jung*. Princeton, New Jersey: Princeton University Press. 1983.

Thomas, Claude Anshin. *At Hell's Gate: A Soldier's Journey from War to Peace*. Boston: Shambhala. 2006.

Wilber, Ken. *A Brief History of Everything*. Boston: Shambhala. 1996.

_____*Grace and Grit: Spirituality and Healing in the Life and Death of Treya Killam Wilber.* Boston: Shambhala. 1993.

About the Author

Following a family tradition of military service (father, James, served in the Marine Corps, and mother, Ruth, in the Navy during World War Two, pictured below in 1944), Michael Orange served in the Marine Corps from 1968 to 1970 including a twelve-month tour of duty in Vietnam where he experienced combat in numerous search-and-destroy missions and patrols. As the squad leader for an 81 mm mortar platoon, he was awarded a meritorious combat promotion to corporal during Operation Durham Peak in the Que Son Mountains. Later he became Section Leader of the Second Section (photo of the author below in Vietnam, 1969).

After his discharge, Mr. Orange witnessed the events immediately precedent to the shootings at Kent State University in 1970, and participated in the famed 1971 march on Washington when for the first time in this country's history, veterans protested against the war they fought and threw their medals back over the Capital fence.

In 2001, he published a memoir of his experiences, *Fire in the Hole: A Mortarman in Vietnam,* and in 2003, Mr. Orange completed nine months of talk therapy for combat-related PTSD. As part of his ongoing recovery (there is no cure), he befriends fellow vets with PTSD, taught a course on the decisions that led to the US involvement in the Vietnam War, and speaks in high schools and colleges about the moral injuries from war. He and his wife, Cynthia, have been active in the peace and justice movements since before they were married in 1973, and with Veterans for Peace since 1991.

After completing four years at Borromeo High School Seminary in Cleveland, Ohio, Mr. Orange earned his B. A. degree from Kent State University in Kent, Ohio (1973) and his M. A. in Urban and Regional Studies from Mankato State University in

Mankato, Minnesota (1979).

Over his seventy-plus years, he has held thirty-four paying jobs including one that lasted thirty years as a city planner for the City of Minneapolis. Past jobs included cook, barber, camp counselor, draftsman, deckhand on a Great Lakes ore carrier, computer programmer, finish carpenter, door-to-door salesman, press operator, railroad laborer ("gandy dancer"), houseparent for delinquent Indian boys, airport planner, and adjunct university professor. Currently, he provides environmental consulting services to the Minnesota Pollution Control Agency and via his company, ORANGE Environmental, LLC. He also loves performing songs from the '60s and '70s at the Minnesota Veterans Home on his 1966, vintage Gibson guitar.

He and his wife, Cynthia, live in St. Paul, Minnesota. Cynthia is the author of five books including two award-winning publications, *Shock Waves: A Practical Guide to Living with a Loved One's PTSD* (2010), and *Take Good Care: Finding Your Joy in Compassionate Caregiving* (2017).

BOOKS BY THIS AUTHOR

Fire in the Hole: A Mortarman in Vietnam

"It is our public responsibility to those who fought the Vietnam War to tell their story to the next generation. It is our responsibility to the children of our veterans to tell the story. Orange has done that and more. . . ."

—Paul Wellstone, United States Senator (deceased)

How does a young man coming of age in the 1960s go from seminarian to soldier? What can scare an average kid from Cleveland into killing for his country? The answer: Vietnam that soul-sucking war that still invades dreams. After surviving a year of combat and the loss of fellow Marines, Orange came home in 1970 to another battlefield Kent State University, where the Ohio National Guard gunned down his classmates. Reeling and confused, he went from soldier to seaman on a Great Lakes ore carrier. Then he became a hippie who fought against the same war he once supported, the same war that stole his youth and innocence.

Orange reflects on his journey of tumult and tears from a vantage point of age and wisdom. This is a survivors tale, told with honesty and compassion for those who fought on both sides of a conflict that sliced through the lives of so many.

[1] *Dream Work*, Jeremy Taylor, Paulist Press, 1983.

[2] J. Michael Orange, *Fire in the Hole: A Mortarman in Vietnam* (Lincoln, NE: Writers Club Press, 2001).

[3] Ibid.

[4] I describe my experiences during the Kent State University anti-war protests and the shooting by the Ohio National Guard in my book, *Fire In the Hole: A Mortarman in Vietnam*.

[5] There is science behind these feelings: "Enabled by the distributed network of the nervous system, different subpersonalities interact dynamically to form the seemingly monolithic but actually fragmented self. For example, one well-known threesome is called the inner child/critical parent/nurturing parent; a related triad is the victim/persecutor/protector. Your nurturing parent-protector subpersonality is reassuring, encouraging, and soothing, and it stands up against the inner and outer voices that are judgmental and demeaning. It does *not* flatter you or make things up. It is grounded in reality, like a solid, caring, no-nonsense teacher or coach who reminds you of good things about you and the world while telling mean people to back off and leave you alone." From *Buddha's Brain: The Practical Neuroscience of Happiness, Love, and Wisdom*, Rick Hanson, Ph.D., Richard Mendius, M.D., 2009, p. 90 (italics in the original).

[6] The Swiss psychologist, Jean Piaget, known for his work on child development, calls this the "concrete operational" and says this is common for six-to-eleven-year-olds.

[7] At the time, I didn't know of the third scripturally embodied person in heaven, Elijah, who "went up by a whirlwind into heaven," 2 Kings 2:11.

[8] For more writings on religion, refer to Chapter 11 "The Passion of a Humanist."

[9] "The Chennault Affair," LBJ Presidential Library, http://www.lbjlibrary.org/mediakits/chennault/

[10] The My Lai Massacre of between 347 and 504 unarmed Vietnamese civilians occurred in March 1968 but was not made public until independent investigative journalist, Seymour Hersh, broke the story in November 1969.

[11] Orange, *Fire in the Hole*.

[12] *Shock Waves: A Practical Guide to Living With a Loved One's PTSD*, Cynthia Orange, 2010.

[13] Unfortunately, these were the healthiest plants in the yard probably due to their constant pruning. My father used to make a "garland of flowers," as one of my siblings called it, as he stripped it of leaves in a single stroke that left a leaf bouquet in his left hand.

[14] The Appendix contains additional related material from Terrance Real's book.

[15] *Broken Toys Broken Dreams: Understanding and Healing Codependency*, Kellogg, Terry, M.A. and Marvel Harrison Kellogg, Ph.D.

[16] *Bradshaw on: The Family. A New Way of Creating Solid Self Esteem*, John Bradshaw.

[17] The story, "Retreat—i have arrived i am home" in Chapter 7 describes my retreat experience.

[18] *At Hell's Gate: A Soldier's Journey from War to Peace*, Claude Anshin Thomas. Interestingly, Claude Thomas describes in his book a retreat he attended in 1991 for veterans led by Thich Nhat Hanh. His experience, including a portentous consultation with Sister Chan Khong, who was an ordained co-leader with Nhat Hahn, resembles the retreat I attended in 2001 with Nhat Hahn. I also had a remarkable consultation with Sister Chan Khong (see the story "Retreat—i have arrived i am home" in Chapter 7). Although we did not know one another at the time, we both witnessed the arrival of the Ohio National Guard on the Kent State University campus in 1970 two days before the Guard shot thirteen students, killing four.

[19] Jessica Orange wrote these poems in her senior year in high school. They were also published in *Fire in the Hole: A Mortarman in Vietnam*.

[20] An excerpted version of this story was published in *Cairns, the Unity Church Journal of the Arts*, Vol. 2, 2010, Unity Church Unitarian, St. Paul, MN.

[21] Recently, science has been able to explain the hormonal mechanics behind the powerful emotions I have for the boys. The key factor is the hormone oxytocin, which promotes nurturing behaviors toward children and bonding in couples. It's associated with blissful closeness and love. It's present in both females and males, though much more so in women. "The human parent-child relationship is unique in the animal kingdom, and it has a singular power to shape how each of us pursues and expresses love as an adult." Source: *Buddha's Brain: The Practical Neuroscience of Happiness, Love & Wisdom*, Rick Hanson, Ph.D., 2009, p. 129.

[22] This story was published in *Cairns, the Unity Church Journal of the Arts*, Vol. 9, 2017, Unity Church Unitarian, St. Paul, MN.

[23] The "historical Jesus" debate has raged for over two hundred years among antiquities scholars in attempts to excavate the man behind the myth. Most (but certainly not all) scholars agree that, at minimum, Jesus probably existed as a blend of the historical, the mythical, and the theological (refer to *On the Historicity of Jesus: Why We Might Have Reason for Doubt*, Richard Carrier, 2014).

[24] Ken Wilber, *Grace and Grit: Spirituality and Healing in the Life and Death of Treya Killam Wilber*, (Boston: Shambhala Press, 2000).

[25] This story continues the practice of changing the actual names of non-public people to honor their privacy. However, Jim Kurtz wanted his name to be used. Jim has joined me each month at the Veterans Home since a few

months after I started in August 2016.

[26] Ken Druck, Ph.D. and James C. Simmons. *The Secrets Men Keep: Breaking the Silence Barrier*. (Garden City, New York: Doubleday and Company, Inc. 1985).

[27] Terrence Real, *I Don't Want to Talk About It: Overcoming the Secret Legacy of Male Depression*. (New York: Simon and Schuster. 1997).

[28] Terry Kellogg, M.A. and Marvel Harrison Kellogg, Ph.D. *Broken Toys Broken Dreams: Understanding and Healing Codependency*. (Lake Kiowa, Texas: B.R.A.T. Publishing. 1990).

[29] John Bradshaw, *Bradshaw on: The Family. A New Way of Creating Solid Self Esteem*. (Deerfield Beach, Florida: Health Communications, Inc. 1988).

[30] Ibid.

[31] Hanson, Rick, Ph.D. and Richard Mendius, M.D. *Buddha's Brain: The Practical Neuroscience of Happiness, Love & Wisdom*.

[32] Bradshaw, op. cit.

[33] Robert Burney, *Codependence: The Dance of Wounded Souls*. (Cambria, California: Joy to You & Me Enterprises. 1995).